53 INTERESTING WAYS OF

HELPING YOUR STUDENTS TO STUDY

Trevor Habeshaw
Pro Assistant Director
(Educational Development)
Bristol Polytechnic

Graham Gibbs
Principal Lecturer, Educational Methods Unit,
Oxford Polytechnic, and Educational Consultant

Sue Habeshaw
Course Advisor & Senior Lecturer
Department of Humanities
Bristol Polytechnic

Technical & Educational Services Ltd
REGISTERED OFFICE
37 Ravenswood Road
Bristol BS6 6BW
UK

ISBN 0 947885 15 3

Price £7.00

About the series

This book is the fourth in the series, Interesting Ways to Teach. Other volumes are:

No 1 53 Interesting things to do in your lectures

No 2 53 Interesting things to do in your seminars and tutorials

No 3 53 Interesting ways to assess your students

No 5 53 Interesting communication exercises for science students.

These books are intended for teachers in further and higher education, though they are equally suitable for nurse tutors, management trainers and instructors on government training projects (PICKUP, JTS etc). Teachers in schools, too, will be able to adapt the material to their own situations.

The purpose of the series is to provide teachers with practical ideas for teaching. While there are sound theoretical justifications for the suggestions (and occasionally even empirical evidence in their support) the emphasis throughout is on practice. The methods have all been tried out, and seen to work, by the authors.

The authors are available as consultants, and to run workshops, in the methods described in the books. Full instructions for do-it-yourself training workshops are also obtainable from the publishers. (The address is at the front of the book.)

Graham.   Sue   Trevor

Acknowledgements

We would like to thank the following for their help and advice in the production of this book:

Jo Corke

John Davidson

Joyce Davies

Vicky Lewis

Adrian Shaw

Contents

TAKING NOTES

WRITING

LEARNING WITH OTHERS

USING THE LIBRARY

REVISING

EXAMS

Introduction

Effective learners are autonomous: they make their own decisions about how, when and what to learn rather than passively following general advice. Hence, there are no right or wrong study techniques. Moreover, students are perfectly capable of discovering what works best for themselves through examining their own experience and that of their colleagues. Effective learning has more to do with awareness and understanding of the purpose and process of learning than with techniques or mechanical skills.

Students do not casually abandon their existing learning methods, which are often deep-rooted habits. Development consists of a gradual evolution of methods based on an understanding of past and present experience.

In these exercises, therefore, there is no attempt to tell students how to study and very little direct advice of any kind. Decision-making is left to students. The purpose of the exercises is to help students to become more reflective, more autonomous and thus more effective learners. Exercises are designed to put students into an informed position from which they can make their own decisions about studying. Where conclusions are drawn they are the conclusions of students themselves. Where techniques are introduced the aim is to offer new experiences and raise awareness rather than to advise all students to use the particular technique.

In the exercises in this book students are encouraged to become observers of their own performance. This will usually be done by their engaging in the process of reflection through thinking and/or writing about their experience. This personal reflection, once completed, is reinforced if they discuss their ideas with one or more of their colleagues - a process which we strongly recommend. Even when very large groups are involved (e.g. 400+), it is still important to arrange for students to discuss their learning with each other. If students are to become autonomous learners, this discussion must be based on a student-centered approach which underplays the role of the teacher.

The group methods which are used most frequently in this book are:

PAIRS

Simply talking things through with someone else enables arguments and ideas to be rehearsed, as well as informing each person about the arguments and ideas of the other.

BUZZ GROUPS

These tend to be rather more structured than simply 'talking things through'. Usually the discussion will concern a specific question or topic which students are asked to consider for a couple of minutes or so. Buzz groups needn't entail any reporting back or pooling of points.

ROUNDS

This is a simple way of ensuring that everyone speaks. In a 'round' everyone, including the teacher, speaks about a given topic. It is helpful if the chairs can be arranged in a circle or horseshoe shape so that everyone can see everyone else. The ground rules which apply in 'rounds' include the following:

- people speak in turn, not out of turn;
- everyone listens when it's not their turn;
- it's OK to repeat what someone else has said.

PYRAMID

The 'pyramid' or 'snowball' method has four stages. First, students work alone. In this way individuals are able to concentrate on clarifying their own views on the matter in hand. Then, in pairs, they share their thoughts or notes with each other. This gives them the opportunity to try out their ideas on someone else. Then groups of four discuss problems, issues, applications etc. which derive from the topic. This then normally leads to some pooling of ideas, conclusions or solutions.

SYNDICATE GROUPS

These are small groups of students, say four to six in number, who work on the same problem, or on different aspects of the same problem, at the same time. On completion of the task each group reports back to the teacher in the hearing of the others so that they can compare other groups' ideas with their own.

BRAINSTORM

In a brainstorm members of the group call out ideas which the teacher lists on a flipchart or board. The ground rules for brainstorming, which have been devised to give group members the freedom to express their ideas, are as follows:

- call out suggestions in any order;
- don't explain or justify your suggestions;
- don't comment on other people's suggestions.

These ways of working are more fully described in the companion volumes in this series:

Gibbs G et al (1987) *53 Interesting things to do in your lectures* for **Buzz groups Item 38** and **Syndicate groups Item 39**, and

Habeshaw S et al (1987) *53 Interesting things to do in your seminars and tutorials* for **Rounds Item 22** and **Pyramid Item 17**.

Materials

Where appropriate we have offered materials to be used as handouts in exercises. Copyright is waived for these materials and you are encouraged to copy them by, for example, using an enlarging photocopier.

It is likely that you will want to edit or rewrite some materials so that they more closely meet the needs of your own students, your college and your course. You are encouraged to make whatever changes will help your students to see the relevance of the exercises. Since it is particularly valuable for students to use subject-specific examples, you are encouraged to collect or write your own materials and to use them in these exercises.

We are always interested to hear from teachers who wish to write to us about their experiences in using the books we write, and especially if their comments help us to make improvements. Meanwhile, good luck with this volume.

Trevor Habeshaw, Graham Gibbs & Sue Habeshaw

Copyright Habeshaw, Gibbs & Habeshaw 1987

14

BEGINNING

Starting off

What do I do in the lecture?

Mottoes

Concentrating

Understanding and remembering

Understanding learning

Self-help groups

Starting off

Students starting a new course are full of anxieties: they are unsure what is expected of them; they are uncertain about how to behave in this strange new environment and they are afraid they won't be able to cope.

Teachers can be helpful by encouraging students to express these anxieties and allowing time for questions and answers about the course.

The varied experience of students arriving to start their new course is such that what may be commonplace to some will be dramatically new to others. A simple way of identifying where the individual difficulties lie is to use a checklist. An example of a checklist follows; you may, however, wish to devise a new one to fit your own situation.

When they have done the exercise, your students may find it useful to keep the checklist for future reference. They could complete it again after a few months to have a visible confirmation of the progress they will certainly have made.

How to run the exercise

a   Hand round copies of 'Exercise: Starting off' and 'Checklist: Starting off'.

b   Keep an eye on the time. Tell the students when to begin and when it is time to move on to each new stage.

c   When they reach stage 4, you will need to chair the question and answer session. Ask each group in turn what their questions are and either answer them yourself or invite other students to suggest answers.

Exercise: Starting off

a   Spend a few minutes on your own completing the checklist, 'Starting off'.

b   Show your completed checklist to your neighbour and spend a couple of minutes each talking about it.

c   Join up with another pair to make a group of four. Go through the list, allocating about three minutes to each item. Anyone in the four who has ticked an item can say why. Anyone who hasn't ticked the item can offer help to those who have. In the last five minutes, note down any questions you would like to ask the teacher or any other member of the class.

d   This will be a question and answer session arising from the 'fours' activity above.

e   In your own time, after the session, make a note of any matters which are particular to you and which you still need to clear up with your teacher.

Checklist: Starting off

This is a list of things which often worry students when they start a new course.
Read the list of statements and tick those which you feel may apply to you. If you wish
to add a comment about any item please do so. If you feel any aspects have been
omitted, please add them at the end.

1   I'm not sure how much work I'll have to do on this course.   ....

2   I'm afraid I'll get behind in my work.   ....

3   I'm worried that I won't know what to write down in lectures.   ....

4   I'm dreading the prospect of writing essays again.   ....

5   I think that I probably won't be a very good student.   ....

6   I don't know how much I'll be expected to read for each subject.   ....

7   I'm not really sure what a seminar is.   ....

8   I hope no-one asks me to speak out in class.   ....

9   I don't want other people to think I'm stupid.   ....

10   I'm not sure what to do if I get into difficulty on the course.   ....

11   _____   ....

12   _____   ....

What do I do in the lecture?

For students starting a new course in further or higher education lecturing is an unfamiliar teaching method. When these students were at school they may have been subjected to dictated notes or uninterrupted talk from their teachers but they have probably never before been in the situation of being expected to listen to the teacher talking for up to an hour, make their own selection of the essential points and note them down coherently without any system for checking that they are doing it right. As well as developing these new skills they will need to adapt them according to the variation in their teachers' lecturing styles. Students with unconventional entry qualifications may have particular problems. This exercise gives students the opportunity to admit to their difficulties in adjusting to the lecture method and to discuss solutions in a supportive group.

How to run the exercise

a   Hand out copies of 'Checklist: What do I do in the lecture?'

b   Give students four or five minutes to work on the statements printed on the sheet and, if they want to, to add their own statements in the spaces provided.

c   Students then spend about ten minutes discussing their comments, either in pairs or in fours, sharing their knowledge and experience. This models good behaviour for any future collaborative activities they may enter into.

d   At the end of the group discussion, move quickly through the statements, commenting from your own perspective on any outstanding issues. This can take as long as is needed to provide the information and to allay any remaining apprehensions.

e   Recommend that students keep their copies of the checklist so that they can look back at them in a few months' time and see how much progress they have made.

Checklist: What do I do in the lecture?

Read the list of statements below and tick those which you feel may apply to you. If you wish to add a comment about any item please do so. If you feel any aspects have been omitted, please add them at the end.

1   I'm not sure what I have to do in the lectures.   ....

2   I'll probably try to write down everything the lecturer says.   ....

3   I'm not sure that I'll know what's important.   ....

4   I don't know how to make sure if I've fully understood what
    the lecturer has said.   ....

5   I'm not sure if it's better to get down as much as I can
    or just make short notes.   ....

6   I don't know what a set of lecture notes looks like.   ....

7   I'm expecting the lecturers to be pretty much the same
    in the way they go about their lecturing.   ....

8   I might join a note-taking 'co-operative' with other students.   ....

9   _____   ....

10 _____   ....

Mottoes

If you ask students to identify the problems which they are meeting or expect to meet on their course, you will find that only some of these difficulties can be solved by the acquisition of study skills: other problems, such as lack of confidence, divided attention or family hostility, require different treatment. This 'mottoes' exercise is based on the two assumptions that students have different problems from each other and that the best person to find the solution is the one who has the problem. This exercise also gives students practice in supporting each other without being intrusive.

How to run the exercise

a   Give students the handouts and ask them to write down three major and three minor problems using the spaces provided.

     (The reason for including minor problems is to ensure that no problem is considered too trivial to mention.)

b   Make a list of problems on the board. If the student group is small, you can include all the problems; if it is large, you can ask each person to contribute just one. (There is no need at this stage to distinguish between major and minor problems.)

c   Organise the list into categories. Though this will clearly depend on your students' choice of problems, there are three categories which are generally found to be useful.

     -   **Information**

       This category includes items such as 'I don't know how to get a locker', 'I don't know what plagiarism is', 'I don't know what "2 ii" means' etc. You can respond to these by either providing the information yourself or telling the students where it is available.

- **Study skills**

  This category includes problems such as 'I don't know how to structure essays', 'I can't keep up in lectures', 'I can't read all the books on the reading list' etc. You can use items in this category as a basis for your study skills programme.

- **Feelings**

  This category covers such items as 'I easily lose heart', 'I panic under pressure', 'I don't know if I'm clever enough for this course' etc. These are problems which lend themselves to treatment by the mottoes exercise.

d   Read through the instructions for the pairs exercise, emphasising the roles of the speaker and the listener. It is helpful if you demonstrate the process beforehand with one of the students.

e   During the exercise it is your responsibility to watch the time and tell the students when ten and twenty minutes are up. If there is an odd number of students in the group, you will need to join in yourself and do the exercise with one of the students.

f   When you have completed the exercise, make a list of everybody's mottoes on the board. (You will find that they have come up with mottoes like 'I can do it!' 'Do it now!' 'Think positive!') Putting together such a cheerful and optimistic list is a positive way to end a class.

Exercise: Mottoes

a Write down THREE MAJOR problems and THREE MINOR problems which you have, or expect to have, on your course. Use the spaces below.

1

2

3

i

ii

iii

b As a group, list the major and minor problems.

c Explore the list to see if any obvious categories emerge.

d Get into pairs and take ten minutes each as speaker and listener.
SPEAKER: Choose one of the problems on the list on the board and take your time to explore it. Speak or be silent as you wish. As you talk, try to find a 'motto' which will help you to deal with the problem for yourself.
LISTENER: Listen. You can help the speaker by asking 'Is that a motto?' from time to time if you think you hear one.

e Each student in turn, going round the class, says 'A motto I've got from this exercise is ....'

Concentrating 4

Students often complain of not being able to concentrate. They say things like 'One minute I'm listening to the lecturer droning on - and the next I'm thinking about something completely different' or 'I can plod my way through a whole chapter we are supposed to read, and when I look back I find I can hardly recognise it, let alone remember what it was all about. My mind is a complete blank'.

To some extent the problem is to do with the way material is presented to students; teachers can usually predict which lectures, and which textbooks, students will find tedious. But more importantly the problem is misconceived. Concentrating is not something which most people can will themselves to do. It is not an inbuilt ability, or even a skill, so much as a by-product of being involved in a task. Situations which encourage this involvement are: those where the goals and purposes are clear; those where students are mentally active (e.g. taking notes, solving problems, answering questions); those where students are encouraged to complete tasks (by means of rewards, deadlines, dividing tasks into small chunks etc.); those which give students background knowledge with which to approach the topic; and, in particular, those which are under the control of the students themselves and are oriented to meeting their goals.

This exercise is designed to help students to recognise for themselves the character-istics of situations in which they find themselves concentrating, or losing concentration, and to share ideas about the implications for their studying.

How to run the exercise

a   Hand round copies of 'Exercise: Concentrating'.

b   Let the students do the exercise unaided. Your job is to provide the equipment

(overhead projector and transparencies), time the stages of the exercise, lead the
plenary discussion and announce the final round.

Exercise: Concentrating

a   Think back to two occasions on which you found yourself not concentrating on your studying. You may have been in a lecture, reading a textbook, or in any other situation. Write down what was going on. Why were you not concentrating? (3 minutes)

b   Now think back to two occasions when you were concentrating really well and completely wrapped up in what you were studying. Write down what situations you were in and why you think you were concentrating. (3 minutes)

c   Get into pairs and describe your experiences to your partner. Ask each other questions about your experiences. If your partner blames boring teachers or boring textbooks for loss of concentration (or puts good concentration down to exciting teachers and exciting books) don't accept this explanation; press your partner for descriptions of what he or she was *doing* at the time when concentration was good or bad. (10 minutes)

d   Join with another pair to make a group of four. As a group write about your experiences on OHP transparencies under the headings:
    'We find that we are concentrating when we.........' and
    'We find that we are not concentrating when we........'
    (20 minutes)

e   Each group in turn displays its OHP transparencies and talks about them. This can lead to a general discussion. (15 minutes)

f   Each student in turn, going round the class, says one thing he or she is going to try doing in future to avoid losing concentration.

Understanding and remembering 5

It is common for students to believe that they are supposed to memorise and remember all their course material. This is not only misguided but actually impossible. Much of what students encounter is meant to be understood rather than memorised. (If it is understood it is in any case far more likely to be remembered in the long term.) Students often need help in recognising what they are supposed to understand and what, if anything, they are supposed simply to memorise.

How to run the exercise

(This is written in the form of a script for the teacher who is running the exercise.)

a   'The content of your course is not all meant to be memorised. Amongst all the information and explanations there will be a few facts which you will have to remember - and you will have to spot which these are. But mostly you will be expected to *understand* what the material is about, so that you can *use* it. (You will also find that if you can understand something, then you will be able to remember it better.)'

b   'Have a look at the handout. It shows some of the things which have to be memorised, and some which have to be understood, in a variety of different subject areas. Can you see the difference? The things to be memorised are mainly names, figures or simple procedures. The things to be understood are things which need explaining, and you need to understand them in order to be able to use them. Try listing ten things you have to memorise and ten you have to understand *from your own course.*' (5 minutes)

c   'Now, in pairs, compare your lists of ten items with your partner.' (5 minutes)

d   'Now, in fours, discuss the following questions:

  1   What items (if any) do you need to memorise before you can understand what the topic is about?

2   What items (if any) do you need to understand before it is possible to make much progress in remembering the details?

3   What sorts of things do you *do* with material when you want to memorise it?

4   What sorts of things do you *do* with material when you want to understand it?' (15 minutes)

e   'Now can we discuss your answers to the questions? Can we start with question 1? Can you give some examples of items which you need to memorise? ...'

Exercise: Understanding and remembering

Subject area	Material for memorising	Material for understanding
Agriculture	Plant names	Why plants are pruned
	Tractor tyre pressures	How a seed drill works
Biochemistry	Names of the amino acids	Structure and function of proteins
	Equation of a reaction	Kinetics of a reaction
Construction	Names of tools	Why concrete mixes vary
	Names of types of brick	Why different types of paint are used
Engineering	Names of parts of a lathe	Purposes of lubrication systems
	Types of lathe	How cutting tools work
History	Dates of events	Causes of events
	Names of Acts of Parliament	Purposes of Acts of Parliament
Literature	Names of characters	What structuralism is
	Dates of publication	How to do a feminist reading of a text

Your 10 items:

Material for memorising   **Material for understanding**

1..   ....

2..   ....

3..   ....

4..   ....

5..   ....

6..   ....

7..   ....

8..   ....

9..   ....

10..   ....

Notes:

Understanding learning

A problem which has been much discussed in the literature on student learning is that of students not understanding what learning itself is. Unsophisticated students seem to believe that learning consists of the accumulation of stores of unconnected factual information. For such students the contestants in the television quiz show *Mastermind* represent the pinnacle of learning. As a result these students approach every learning task as if it involved reproducing each element of the subject matter in its every detail. All tasks are seen as memorisation tasks, and they do not try to make sense of what they are trying to memorise. When they write answers to questions they try to convey as many facts as possible, and they expect marks to be awarded accordingly.

This exercise is designed to help such students to realise that the purpose of learning is the construction of meaning, that the purpose of communicating is the communication of meaning, and that marks are awarded (or at least they should be!) for communicating meaning successfully. Since explaining or discussing this issue seems to have very little effect, the exercise is designed to give students an experience which demonstrates it.

How to run the exercise

a   Get students to sit back to back in pairs in such a way that one of each pair is facing a screen and the other is facing the other way. Each pair should be far enough away from other students not to be able to see or hear what they are doing.

b   Say to the students facing the screen, 'For the next five minutes you must not talk, and your partner, facing the other way, must not look round or talk. In a moment I am going to display an image on the screen. You will have five minutes in which to learn this image. You may practise drawing it, take notes, and do anything you like to learn it except move from your seat or talk. When five minutes are up I will remove the image and you must put away your notes. You will then have to get your partner to draw the image.'

c   Display the image which follows; this is easiest with an overhead projector so that the room doesn't have to be darkened. You may need to remind students not to talk or look round.

d   Say to the students facing the screen, 'Now please put your notes away. You are to get your partner to draw the image. You must stay back to back, and not turn round to see what your partner is drawing. Don't talk to anyone except your partner. Talk quietly so that no-one else can hear. The people facing away from the front must not talk, even to ask or answer questions - you must simply draw what you are told. You have five minutes.'

e   At the end of five minutes all the drawings should be displayed on the walls so that everyone can see and discuss them.

f   Ask the students what strategies they adopted as 'learners' and as 'teachers'.

(You will find that, as 'learners', a few students perceived the image as a horse, with a rider, facing to the right. For them the task was easy. A few will have tried hard to see a meaningful image and some of them will have been successful. The others will all have tried to memorise what was apparently a meaningless collection of black shapes.

When trying to 'teach' the image to their partners, most of this last group will have taken a technical approach, e.g. 'There are 27 blobs inside a frame. I'm going to tell you where to put them ....' or 'Draw a box 10 cms square and divide it into 9 equal boxes. Divide the top left box into two vertically. In the left hand of these boxes you should draw two blobs, one the vertical mirror image of the other ....')

g   Ask students which of the drawings are good representations of the image.

(You will find that they will reject all the 'blob' drawings, however carefully constructed. They will approve of the drawings of horses, even if they look nothing like the original image. Even stick drawings, half the proper size, and facing the wrong way, will be judged as better than a blob drawing of exactly the right dimensions, with virtually all the blobs in the right place, but which does not convey 'horseness'.)

h   Encourage students to identify the implications of this exercise for learning in general.

(These are:

- if you are trying to find meaning, or make sense of information, learning can be effortless and successful. But if the information is meaningless, it's very difficult to learn anything;

- communicating with another person can be very easy and successful if you are concentrating on communicating meaning. No matter how much information you have, if you cannot get across the overall meaning of the message - preferably at the start - then your communication will probably fail;

- you are judged on how much you have learned by the extent to which the overall meaning is conveyed, rather than on the accumulation of details, however accurate these details are.)

i   Encourage students to identify the applications of this exercise to their studying. (For example, students should be aiming to make sense of their lectures and come away with notes which encapsulate the meaning, rather than trying to record and memorise the entire content. And when they come to transform lecture notes into an essay they should extract the key ideas rather than regurgitate the information.)

Once these analogies have been grasped by students, it is then easy subsequently to refer to 'the horse and rider' to remind students of what their real task is in various learning situations.

Self-help groups 7

Your students can be suprisingly isolated. They probably don't see you very often and may not have many opportunities to talk to each other about their work. This has implications for their motivation as well as their understanding of the subject. The answer is for them to arrange to meet as a self-help group.

Self-help groups are simply informal groups of students who meet without a teacher to help each other with their learning. They were developed in the context of distance-learning systems such as the Open University, but they can be equally valuable in conventional contexts.

What you can do

1   Talk to your class about the idea of self-help groups. Ask their permission to circulate a list of their addresses and phone numbers.

2   Hold a meeting specifically to put your students in touch with each other or put fifteen minutes aside during your first meeting with them so that they can swop addresses etc.

3   Suggest activities which they could undertake on their own without you.

4   Act as postperson for communications between your students - for example, by putting up a notice board outside your office - to help publicise self-help group meetings and pass on messages.

5   Tell the students where and when they can contact you to clear up any problems.

6   Put aside a few minutes at the start of classes to answer outstanding queries from recent self-help group meetings, or ask groups to report briefly on what happened.

7   Give students advice on how to run their self-help groups. The handout, 'Running a self-help group', can be distributed and discussed in class.

Running a self-help group

At school you were probably told that getting help from someone else was cheating. In fact it can be very beneficial to your learning to be able to ask for help when you need it. And giving help is also useful: there is no better way of learning something than trying to teach it to someone else! Here are some guidelines for setting up a self-help group so that you will have other people to help you with your learning.

a   Don't assume that someone else will set up a group for you. Do it yourself !

b   Make sure that everyone in your group has everyone else's name and phone number or address.

c   At the first meeting, spend some time introducing yourselves: say who you are, what your interests are, why you are doing the course, what you want to get out of the group etc. Make sure you can put a face to the names you may want to contact later on.

d   Choose a 'leader' or chairperson - someone who takes responsibility for arranging the meetings and cancelling them if something goes wrong.

e   Never finish a meeting without arranging the next one. It is harder to fix a time and place to suit everyone if you are not all together.

f   Regular meetings (e.g. every Tuesday at 11 am in the Students' Union coffee bar) are easier to remember, and will get better attendance, than meetings at irregular times and places.

g   Try to plan ahead. If you can agree on a topic beforehand, people will know what to expect and be able to prepare for the meeting.

h   However organised you are, always allow time for general chat, even if this isn't anything to do with the course. Although your time may be precious, the purpose of self-help groups is partly social. If you get too efficient, you may stop enjoying the meetings.

i   Self-help groups don't have to be big: two people can meet together very productively.

j   Self-help groups are particularly useful for revision if you have exams at the end of your course. Divide the course topics into sections and share these out between you. Each member of the group can revise one of the sections, present an overview to the group and then answer any questions.

k   You can also use self-help group meetings to sort out queries about the course, to exchange ideas and books before writing essays, to work on activities which demand a group of students gathered together, and generally to improve your learning skills. Your teacher will have a variety of exercises to help you with this.

l   If your group can't sort out a problem on its own, ask a teacher as soon as possible.

PLANNING

The next five minutes

Planning your week

This term

Planning a project

Reviewing

The next five minutes 8

It can be useful to students to examine in fine detail the way they plan and spend even short periods of study time. If sizeable tasks can be broken up into small components then short time slots can be used effectively. If, however, tasks are perceived as monumental (e.g. 'a 3,000-word essay which will take at least 20 hours') then short time slots are likely to be filled by extended coffee breaks and work will be delayed.

This exercise is designed to help students to organise themselves so as to make efficient use of their study time.

How to run the exercise

a   Say to the students, 'Imagine that I can give you an extra hour to do some studying in, starting in three minutes. In the next three minutes, note down how you are going to use that hour'.

b   After three minutes get the students to form groups of three and say, 'Compare your plans. How detailed are they? Have you just written "Do some reading for my essay" or have you written something more specific, such as "Read p105 onwards of Bloggs until I can understand about x, and then write section 3 of my essay"?'

c   Invite groups to contribute examples of plans and make comments.

d   Say to the students, 'Now you can have just five minutes' study time , starting in two minutes. What can you usefully plan to do in five minutes so that you don't waste this opportunity? Note down your plans, individually'.

e   After two minutes ask the students to form groups of three again and compare their plans.

f   When they have done this, say to them, 'I can now give you a block of four hours in which to study. Plan out in detail how you could effectively use this time, drawing up a timetable made up of eighteen ten-minute slots. You have ten minutes to do this and you can confer with a neighbour if this will help you.'

g   After ten minutes ask the students to form groups of three again and explain their plans to the other people in the group.

h   Ask the group to discuss the following questions:

(you could write these on an OHP transparency)

1   Would it be useful to plan your longer study sessions at the start rather than just plunging straight in (as in the three minutes/one hour exercise)?

2   Would it be useful always to have a five- or ten-minute task handy in case opportunities arise, on the bus, between classes etc?

3   Would it be useful to have at hand a list of tasks which need doing, broken up into small enough bits to enable you to do the kind of planning you have been asked to do here?

i   Invite students to contribute to an open discussion.

Planning your week

9

The organisation of study time is a key skill for students to acquire: there is plenty of evidence that organised students do better than disorganised students. This exercise increases students' awareness of how they are spending their time at present and provides them with a rational basis for planning changes in how they set their priorities and allocate their time.

How to run the exercise

a   Give students the handout, 'Exercise: Planning your week', together with the chart, a week before you run the exercise. It is worthwhile supervising their initial completion of the chart for the part of 'today' that has already elapsed: once they have started recording their activities they are more likely to continue.

b   The following week, get students to analyse their charts by answering a selection of the following questions. Encourage them to compare their answers with each other and discuss differences. (15 minutes)

1   How many hours did you put in last week? How many hours are expected of you on the course, and how many hours do your friends do?

2   How many hours did you spend in class last week, and how many out of class?

3   Of the hours spent out of class, how many did you spend doing work for assessment and how many on work you chose to do for yourself?

4   How many hours did you spend reading?

5   How many hours did you spend in preparation for, and how many following up, class activities?

6   Of your private study time, what proportion was in the morning, and what proportion in the afternoon or evening? When are you at your best: morning

or evening?

7   How many hours did you spend on the different parts of your course, or on the different subjects you are taking? Which subjects do you like best? Which subjects are you best at? Which subjects do you think you need to spend most time on to ensure you will do well?

8   How many hours do you think you 'wasted' during the week?

9   What was the average length of your private study periods? (Divide your total private study time by the number of times you had private study periods.) How long can you work before needing a short break?

c   Give students five minutes to write down their conclusions about how they spent the previous week. You can read them this example if you think it is needed.

'I worked less hard than I thought I did. I spent almost all my time on one of my courses and practically none on the others. I spent more time eating, drinking coffee and drinking beer than I did studying. I work very badly late at night and find it hard to concentrate, and yet 75% of all my private study was after 10 pm. I try to work in long stints - my average was nearly 2 hours - but in fact I feel like a break after about 45 minutes: I might be better off planning shorter sessions. Practically everything I did was to do with catching up or responding to demands made on me - I don't seem to be planning ahead, preparing for things or thinking about revision.'

d   Give the students five minutes to write down all the things they would *like* to do in the coming week, academically and socially.

e   When they have written these, ask them to plan the coming week in detail, specifying exactly what they intend to do at what time. These plans can be briefly explained to a partner who asks questions and helps to clarify the plan. Make it clear that these should be plans which they seriously want to keep to: there is little point in devising an idealised and impossible scheme of work. (15 minutes) f   Ask students to keep a full diary during the following week.

g   A further session can be held in which students analyse their second week's diary and compare it with both their previous week's chart and their plan. Differences can be discussed, with particular emphasis on occasions when work was avoided or priorities distorted.

Exercise: Planning your week

Use the chart to note down what you do for a whole week. Start right now and fill in everything you have done so far today.

a   Try to be as detailed as possible: a fifteen-minute slot, for example, can be very valuable to your studying.

b   Try to be as informative as possible: it is important to specify which part of your course you are spending time on and whether you are doing, for example, 'additional' reading, or 'compulsory' reading for a piece of assessed work.

c   Don't just fill in things to do with your studying: the time you spend sitting in the coffee bar or watching television is all part of the picture of how you spend your time.

d   Keep the chart with you and fill it in regularly and often (or you will forget what you have been doing).

	Mon	Tues	Wed	Thurs	Fri	Sat	Sun
8 am							
9 am							
10 am							
11 am							
12 noon							
1 pm							
2 pm							
3 pm							
4 pm							
5 pm							
6 pm							
7 pm							
8 pm							
9 pm							
10 pm							
11 pm							
12 midnight							
1 am							

This term

This exercise is concerned with longer term planning than the exercise in item 9. It is intended to help students to prioritise and spread their work so as to meet deadlines, and still leave time clear for activities such as background reading and revision.

Students can undertake the exercise on their own, but they may benefit from doing it with at least one other student from the same course. The exercise is very straightforward: it consists of identifying everything that needs to be done and mapping it onto a plan of the term so that the pattern of work can be seen at a glance.

How to run the exercise

a   Give students copies of the handouts.

b   Ask them to fill in Handout 1. Suggest to them that if they don't know the answers, they can find them out from each other, from you or from the course guide.

c   Ask students to check their dates with a partner.

d   Ask them to fill in Handout 2 as follows:

'Firstly, write in every date and deadline you know about.

Now write in sensible target *completion* dates for your main tasks such as handing in set work. Then estimate how long these tasks will take you. For example, you might expect an essay to take you ten days from start to finish, and a lab report three days.

Work backwards from your deadlines to establish when you will need to *start* on your main tasks. If you find you have several things on at once you may need to start one of them earlier to get it out of the way. Aim to distribute your workload evenly across the term, and to leave yourself enough time later on for things such as revision.'

e   Ask students to compare plans for the term with their partners.

f   Introduce a round in which each student in turn completes the sentence 'One thing I have made a decision about is to ....'

g   Planning is an on-going process, so you could suggest that students refer regularly to their plans to remind them of their intentions, and change them as circumstances alter. You could also ask students for suggestions as to how to continue the planning process as the term progresses.

Handout 1: Events and deadlines

Write down the dates of the following events this term:

	Course 1	Course 2	Course 3	Course 4
Course Title:				
Exam(s)				
Essay deadline(s)				
Laboratory report deadline(s)				
Seminar presentations				
Field trips/visits				
Project report or exhibition deadlines				
Bank holidays or other 'days off'				
Other events (specify)				

	Mon	Tues	Wed	Thurs	Fri	Sat	Sun
Week 1							
Week 2							
Week 3							
Week 4							
Week 5							
Week 6							
Week 7							
Week 8							
Week 9							
Week 10							
Week 11							
Week 12							

Longer term deadlines:

Planning a project 11

Project work can be very valuable for students: it encourages them to take an interest in critical enquiry, and to develop research techniques and problem solving skills. In particular it requires them to take responsibility for their own learning. This may cause difficulties, however: students may be unused to working alone and unclear about the new relationship with their supervisor.

The supervisor and the student need to clarify their roles and decide how responsibilities will be allocated. They also need to work out a plan for the project and agree on a schedule.

What you can do

1   Talk with your student about the roles of the supervisor and supervisee and compare your expectations of the relationship. You will need to agree how far your separate responsibilities extend: how much advice the supervisor is able and willing to give, which decisions the student must make for herself etc. You may like to draw up this agreement formally as a contract so that you are both absolutely clear about the arrangements. An example of an actual contract follows.

Trevor and Pennie will agree the objectives of the project;

Trevor will give advice on literature search;

Trevor will give advice on experimental design;

Pennie is responsible for contacting relevant agencies;

Pennie is responsible for the design of the questionnaire;

Pennie will produce the final draft by May 26th;

Pennie is entitled to the equivalent of 30 minutes' supervision each week.

2 Ask your student to identify the stages of the project and draw up a programme for herself. If she needs help you can show her an example, such as the one below, for comparison. Encourage her to set herself a realistic deadline for each stage of the programme.

Handout: Stages of a technological project

Stage 1 Definition of problem situation
 a awareness of the existence of a problem;
 b analysis of a problem situation;
 c determination of constraints to solution;
 d production of a brief statement of the problem.

Stage 2 Generation of solutions
 a brainstorming possible solutions;
 b amplification of possible solutions.

Stage 3 Collection of information: *requiring*
 a knowledge of sources of relevant information;
 b ability to create information by experimentation;
 c opportunity to collect information.

Stage 4 Organisation of information: *requiring*
 a comprehension of the collected data;
 b knowledge of theory and structure of the subject matter.

Stage 5 Analysis of the information: *involving*
 a interpretation of, and possible extrapolation from, the collected information;
 b breakdown of material into its constitutent parts to be reformed to give a new structure and meaning;
 c rejection of irrelevant information.

Stage 6 Evaluation of proposed solutions: *requiring*
a judgement of the proposed solutions with respect to the imposed constraints amd other criteria of effectiveness.

Stage 7 Statement outlining selected solution
possibly a single solution or a number of solutions with their associated advantages and disadvantages.

Stage 8 Planning the project

Stage 9 Detailed design: *consisting of one or more of...*
a   detailed drawings, specifications and costings;
b   hardware production schedule;
c   specification of proposed schedule or procedure.

Stage 10 Production: *consisting of one or more of ...*
a   manufacture and testing of hardware;
b   supervision of manufacture and testing;
c   production of material (paperwork) relating to any proposed schedule or procedure which is necessary for implementation.

Stage 11 Incorporation of solution into problem situation *possibly requiring...*
a   considerable on-site testing with any subsequent redesign and/or production;
b   instruction of workers operating in the problem situation.

Stage 12 Evaluation of changed situation
a   determination of the extent to which the solution solves the problem;
b   appraisal of any adverse effects caused by the implementation of the solution;
c   decision on the actual working success of the solution when any adverse effects are taken into account;
d   definition of any new or remaining problem(s).

Stage 13 Communication of findings *consisting of one or more of ...*

a complete report of all project stages;

b summary report of important factors;

c folder of material collected during the project;

d oral report possibly involving lecture, interview, viva, audio-visual presentation;

e patent applications, aids to selling, implementation strategies, related problem areas to which the solutions may be applied, remaining work to be done, other applications etc.

Reviewing 12

Your students can get very depressed from time to time if they feel that, despite their efforts, they seem to be making little progress with their studying. Reading, writing essays, even understanding the material, may appear to be no easier now than they were two terms ago. The middle term of an academic year and the middle year of a conventional degree programme find students in an especially vulnerable position. They are far enough away from the beginning for the early euphoria to have faded away and too far away from the end to feel they have a goal to aim for.

What you can do

1   You can help your students at such times by asking them to review their work on the course so far. They will be able to get a better perspective on their working year if, for example, you display the outline of the year's work on an OHP transparency, indicating how much has been accomplished so far and what remains to be done. You can also introduce a few past exam questions and demonstrate to the students how much they already know.

2   You can invite your students to engage in a gentle exercise of self-appraisal. If they have kept their checklists from the early weeks in the course (**see 1 Starting off** and **2 What do I do in the lecture?**), you can set time aside for them to look at them and to remind themselves how far they have come.

3   You can run a structured exercise in which students review their progress.

How to run the exercise

a   Hand round copies of 'Exercise: Reviewing'.

b   Your job is to time the stages of the exercise, draw up the brainstorm list and announce the final round.

Exercise: Reviewing

a   The group brainstorms on answers to the question, 'What does it take/What do you need to be able to do to be a successful student on this course?' Draw up, on the board or on flipchart sheets, a list of personal skills, study skills etc. which will help students to succeed on this course. (5 minutes)

b   Each student takes a piece of A4 lined paper and divides it into three sections. Using the 'brainstorm' list if you want to, fill in each section using the following headings:

- Things that I couldn't do when I started that I now feel quite confident about....
- Things that I couldn't do when I started that I can do now if I make the effort....
- Things that I need to pay particular attention to in the near future....

(10 minutes)

c   Each student in turn, going round the group, specifies: 'One thing I feel confident about; one thing I can do if I try; one thing I'm going to work on'.

READING

Reading lists

SQ3R

Reading flexibly

Reading a journal article

Rip it up

Reading lists

13

Reading lists can be terrifying. Confronted with long lists of titles, students soon realise that they can't possibly read all the books and they panic.

They need to be reassured that they are not expected to read everything on the list. And they need to be helped to develop strategies for making a sensible selection of books.

This exercise encourages them to find ways of coping with reading lists so that they will not be overawed by them.

How to run the exercise

a   Ask your students to bring one of their reading lists to the class. (Have some spares available in case some of them forget.)

b   Explain to them that they don't need to try to read all the books on the list.

c   Suggest that they find ways of prioritising the books on the list, crossing out those which they definitely won't read, bracketing the doubtful ones and marking the others A, B, C etc. in order of importance or usefulness. (Allow about 5 - 10 minutes for this.)

d   Ask them what criteria they use to make their decisions. (You will find that the kinds of reasons they had for prioritising certain books were, for example, that the author's name was familiar to them, the book was often referred to by their teachers, it had been recommended by another student, it was more up to date than others on the list, the word 'introduction' or 'advanced' in the title suggested that it was pitched at the right level etc.) List these reasons on the board.

e   If some students still feel unable to cope with their reading lists, encourage them to go back to the people who wrote them and ask for advice. They may also like to set up reading co-operatives with other students on the same course.

f   This exercise may lead to discussion about the availability of books in the library. Students may claim that reading lists are pointless because the books are always out on loan. This will give you the opportunity to encourage them to investigate the procedure for reserving books and borrowing on inter-library loan and short-term loan.

SQ3R

14

Many students have difficulty coping with set reading because they are not practised in the skills of selecting what they need from a text. SQ3R is a technique which helps unskilled readers to read to more purpose. The handout which follows explains the technique.

How to run the exercise

(If you have never used SQ3R yourself, you would be well advised to try it out before telling your students about it.)

a   Ask students to read the handout.

b   Select a piece of reading for students to use in this exercise: a journal article, for example, or a chapter from a textbook. (A literary text is not suitable, however, as it demands close reading.)

c   Say to the group, 'We are going to try out SQ3R now. The first thing to do is to survey chapter 3 [or whatever]. Just have a quick look and find out what it's about. I'll give you two minutes for this'.

d   Then say to the group, 'The second thing to do is to question. Write down the questions you will be able to answer when you have read the chapter properly. In five minutes we'll have a look at the different questions people have thought of'.

e   Use a round to get students to read out one of the questions they have written down. Stress that there are no right answers and that different people will want to get different things out of their reading. These may also be different from what the author intends.

f   Ask the group to read the chapter, with the aim of answering their questions. Give them a time limit (e.g. 15 minutes). Tell them that if they find they can answer their questions within this time, they should set themselves further, and perhaps more detailed, questions to answer in the remaining time.

g   Ask the group to write down the answers to their questions *from memory* without looking back at the chapter.

h   Now ask them to look back at the chapter to check that their answers were right, and to note down where they feel they need to do more reading or other studying.

i   Have a discussion about SQ3R: ask your students whether they think it looks like a useful technique, reassure them that it gets easier with practice and encourage them to try it out in the normal course of their studying.

You have probably had the experience, when reading, of realising that you have turned over the last few pages without taking anything in. You thought you were concentrating but looking back at what you were supposed to have read you find you can hardly recognise anything after the first page! This doesn't mean you can't concentrate, or can't read, or have a memory like a sieve. It happens to everybody. It is very common for people's minds to go into neutral as early as thirty seconds after starting to read a textbook. It usually happens when they sit down with no other reason for reading than the thought, 'I really must read some more of this ....'

The problem is caused by not reading *actively*. But being active when reading doesn't just happen; it has to be planned for. SQ3R is a simple method of planning your reading so that it is more active, more purposeful, and much more productive.

SQ3R stands for :

Survey   Question   Read   Recall   Review

Survey
Have a quick look through the book (or chapter, or article) to see what it is about and what you can expect to get out of it. You may also find it helpful to survey the list of contents and the index.

Question
Write down the questions you will be able to answer when you have read the book (or

chapter, or article) properly. The survey you have just done, and your own needs (and maybe assignment titles and exam questions) will help you to formulate the questions.

Read

Once you have got some useful questions, reading is easy. All you have to do is find where the answers to your questions are and read those bits carefully, perhaps making a few notes, sketching one or two diagrams, doing some calculations to make sure you understand them, and so on. As soon as you have answered all your questions, get out of the book as soon as you can. Books have a habit of sucking in the unwary and wasting their time. Don't read any more than you absolutely have to!

Recall

Try to answer all your questions without looking at the book or your notes. You'll soon find out what you have learned and what you need to spend more time on.

Review

Go back to the book to check that your answers are right. Go over the things you have got wrong or couldn't answer. Don't get trapped by the book again! Just dip into the relevant bits.

Reading flexibly

15

It is quite common for students to think that studying would be easy if only they could read fast enough. There are widespread beliefs about amazing techniques which somehow spread your eyes so that you can see whole pages at a glance, control eye movements so that you have to look at fewer places on a page to read it, or which simply accelerate reading to supernatural speeds. These techniques are not generally effective because eye movements are controlled by our need to make sense of what is on the page and attempts to control eye movements interfere with our ability to make sense of what we read. And the faster we read, the less we get out of reading. The American comedian Woody Allen once told that he took a speed reading course which taught him to read by glancing down an imaginary line in the middle of each page. He said, 'I read *War and Peace* in twenty minutes. It's about Russia'.

In reality effective reading is about being flexible and purposeful.

This is an exercise designed to help students to become more aware of flexibility and purposefulness in reading.

How to run the exercise

(This is written in the form of a script for the teacher who is running the exercise.)

a   'There are two lists on the top part of the handout. The one on the left is a list of different types of reading material. The one on the right is a list of different ways of reading. Match the pairs which go together by joining them with a line.'

b   'Now you have three minutes to compare your answers with your neighbour.' (Deal with any questions before continuing.)

c   'Your course requires a whole range of different kinds of reading for different purposes. You certainly won't get far if you try to read everything as if it was a novel! On the bottom part of the handout, list all the different kinds of material you will be reading, and then describe how you will go about reading each type. You have ten minutes for this.'

d   'Now get into groups of four and compare your lists. Draw up a combined list, using all the ideas from your group of four.'

e   'I would like a member from each group of four, in turn, to write on the board one of the types of reading material they have listed and to write next to it how they intend to read it. Other groups can comment on similarities or differences in their own lists.' (This can lead into general discussion of the importance of flexibility in reading.)

Handout: Reading flexibly

Type of reading material	Type of reading
Sports page of the newspaper	Plotting a route
Instructions on the side of a packet	Looking up facts
Science fiction novel	Quick scan to find a result
A - Z map of Birmingham	Slow step by step reading
Complete British Rail timetable	Repeated reading, thinking and re-reading
Table of library opening hours	Repeated reading and reciting from memory
Technical photography manual	Fast reading without effort for hours
Crossword clues	Scan quickly to get going, referring to sections as you go along
Rules of the game Monopoly	A quick glance and pin it to the wall for reference
Poem in a school poetry book	Careful slow reading of selected sections and noting things down

Type of reading material	How you will read it
1	
2	
3	
4	
5	
6	
7	
8	
9	
10	

Reading a journal article

16

Teachers are good at getting the most they can from journal articles in as short a time as possible and, knowing their importance, are inclined to flavour their reading lists with references which direct students to the journal section of the library.

Students will benefit from developing an approach to the reading of journal articles which is both effective and speedy. They need a procedure to follow which highlights the importance of both the content of the article and its correct citation. Teachers can help by offering a simple format for them to follow while they get used to dealing with journals. One such *pro forma* is included here. While it was written to meet the needs of social science students, it offers a model upon which teachers in other disciplines could base their own version.

The test of any aid of this kind is its continued use by students. If they find it helpful, they will continue to use it in this or some modified version which suits them better. It is in fact this development of a personal style which most helps students to attain independence as learners.

How to run the exercise

a   Give students an offprint of a journal article and a copy of the handout. They will find it helpful if you spend a little time going through the form with them, answering their questions and offering any clarification they may need.

b   Ask them to read the article and then answer the questions in the handout.

c   Get them to compare what they have written in pairs or small groups. Any problems which arise can be discussed by the class as a whole.

d   Encourage students to use this *pro forma* or a similar one in their future work.

a Full reference

Journal _____

_____

Year _____

Volume _____

Number _____

Library reference _____

Author _____

Title _____

_____

b Comments

1 The problem
    What is the problem?

2 Introduction
    What does the literature survey tell you about the author's frame of reference?
    What are the author's hypotheses?
    What major references are cited?

3 Method

What techniques were used? How adequate are they?

Are there any obvious measures of reliability/validity?

What are the major dependent and independent variables?

4 Subjects

How was the sample size/ bias/matching arrived at?

5 Results

What statistical techniques are used?

How are the results analysed?

6 Discussion and conclusions

Summary of findings:

- major:
- subsidiary:

Evaluation of the article:

- strong points:
- other points:
- things you disagree with:

Rip it up 17

Literate people frequently have a respect for books which borders on reverence. They can be appalled by the sight of someone writing in a book, tearing out chapters or even bending back the spine to open the pages out fully.

Yet this person is simply trying to use the book effectively.

Books, as learning aids, are often poorly designed and difficult to use. It requires considerable effort on the part of the reader to overcome the limitations which arise from the structure of the book itself. For example, while books are increasingly expensive, student texts are usually printed on cheap paper, poorly bound, and produced in small print with narrow lines and margins.

Teachers can help students to see that undue reverence for books can have negative learning consequences and encourage them not to feel guilty about ways in which they try to access the information in their books. They can point out that the very fact that books are so expensive means that any strategy which helps students to learn from them must be worthwhile in economic, as well as in educational, terms.

How to run the exercise

a   Take a book into the classroom with you and rip it up in front of the students: pull off the cover and separate some of the pages. (You probably won't need to ask the students how they feel about this: a number of them will have responded to your action with horrified gasps.)

b   Ask them to explain why they have this reverence for books and encourage them to challenge their own feelings of fear and guilt.

c   Ask them to think of ways in which they can personalise their own texts so as to make them more friendly and accessible as learning aids. For example, underlining, highlighting, boxing, writing notes and using colours (as well as ripping up the books) should be encouraged as students develop their own style as effective learners.

TAKING NOTES

Why take notes?

Taking notes from books

Taking notes in lectures

Five teachers

Using patterns

Sharing notes

Why take notes? 18

If you ask students why they are taking notes in a lecture there will often be a moment's pause while they struggle to find a reason: 'Well, I suppose I'll need them for revision, won't I?' In fact students' notes are often not much use for any particular purpose because they didn't have any particular purpose in mind when they were taking them which meant that they had no basis for being selective.

This exercise is designed to encourage students to think about their purpose in taking notes so that they can select and record only those elements which meet this purpose.

How to run the exercise

a   Have a ten-minute lecture prepared. (This can be part of the course you are teaching the students, or a talk on a topic of general interest.) Alternatively, you can use an audiotape or videotape.

b   Divide the class into four groups of students and give each group different instructions about what they should do while listening to the lecture.
Note: Don't let the different groups know what the others are supposed to be doing.

c   Instruct the groups as follows:
Group 1 'You should listen and take notes. At the end of the lecture you will be tested for key factual information by a multiple choice question test'.
Group 2 'You should listen and take notes. At the end you will be asked to write a three hundred-word summary of the lecture'.
Group 3 'You should listen and take notes. At the end you will be asked to form groups of four and discuss the lecture for ten minutes. There will be no assessment and I will not take part in your discussion'.

Group 4 'I have no special instructions for you'.

d   After the lecture, explain to the students that they will not be required to do a test, write a summary or discuss the lecture. Instead, take one student from each group to form groups of four who then compare the types of notes they have taken and explain what they were listening for during the lecture.

e   Ask groups to pool these differences in a plenary discussion. You should aim to bring out two main points:

- if you know what you want notes for before you start writing them, this will help you to concentrate in the lecture and select what is relevant to your purpose;

- the type of notes you take should depend on, and vary with, the use to which you intend to put them.

f   You can vary this exercise by dividing the class into two groups and giving one group an exam question. Tell this group that the lecture will be on that topic. Tell the other group nothing about the lecture or about assessment. This will help students to realise that listening to a lecture with a specific question in mind is much easier, and results in better notes, than listening without anything to guide their thinking.

Taking notes from books 19

A common mistake which students make when taking notes from books is that they attempt to write down everything, if not in full at least in summary form. This exercise encourages them to be selective in their note-taking in the hope that they will have the confidence to leave out irrelevancies in the future.

The passage used in this exercise is particularly appropriate for students of social science, social work, nursing etc. Equally suitable passages for other disciplines are not difficult to find.

How to run the exercise

a   Give your students a copy of a selected extract, or refer them to a passage in their course textbook, and ask them to make notes in preparation for an essay for which the particular piece of reading will be relevant. (For our sample extract, a suitable title might be 'The relevance of the theory of the Oedipus Complex to psychology/social work/health visiting etc. today'.)

b   Ask them what they have selected as relevant and what they have discarded. There is also an opportunity here to discuss other aspects of note-taking such as the use of quotations (e.g. of key definitions) and lists and subheadings. (For our sample extract, suitable subheadings could be 'Definition; Influence; Recommendations'.)

c   Now ask your students to make notes in preparation for an essay with a different title. (For our sample extract, a suitable second title might be 'The relevance of the theory of the Oedipus Complex to the study of literature today'.)

d   Ask them to compare their notes for the literature essay with their notes for the social science essay.

e   This can be followed up with a discussion on taking notes selectively and perhaps further practice: you can ask students to repeat the procedure with a passage of their choice or review a set of past notes in the light of what they have learned from this exercise.

The Oedipus Complex

...The child's first choice of an object, which derives from its need for help, claims our further interest. Its choice is directed in the first instance to all those who look after it, but these soon give place to its parents. Children's relations to their parents, as we learn alike from direct observation of children and from later analytic examination of adults, are by no means free from elements of accompanying sexual excitation. The child takes both of its parents, and more particularly one of them, as the object of its erotic wishes. In so doing, it usually follows some indication from its parents, whose affection bears the clearest characteristics of a sexual activity, even though of one that is inhibited in its aims. As a rule a father prefers his daughter and a mother her son; the child reacts to this by wishing, if he is a son, to take his father's place, and, if she is a daughter, her mother's. The feelings which are aroused in these relations between parents and children and in the resulting ones between brothers and sisters are not only of a positive or affectionate kind but also of a negative or hostile one. The complex which is thus formed is doomed to early repression; but it continues to exercise a great and lasting influence from the unconscious. It is to be suspected that, together with its extensions, it constitutes the *nuclear complex* of every neurosis, and we may expect to find it no less actively at work in other regions of mental life. The myth of King Oedipus, who killed his father and took his mother to wife, reveals, with little modification, the infantile wish, which is later opposed and repudiated by the *barrier against incest.* Shakespeare's *Hamlet* is equally rooted in the soil of the incest-complex, but under a better disguise.

...It is inevitable and perfectly normal that a child should take his parents as the first objects of his love. But his libido should not remain fixated to these first objects; later on, it should merely take them as a model, and should make a gradual transition from them on to extraneous people when the time for the final choice of an object arrives. The detachment of the child from his parents is thus a task that cannot be evaded if the young individual's social fitness is not to be endangered. During the time at which repression is making its selection among the component instincts, and later, when there should be a slackening of the parents' influence, which is essentially responsible for the expenditure of energy on these repressions, the task of education meets with great problems, which at the present time are certainly not always dealt with in an understanding and unobjectionable manner.

Freud S (1976)   'Five lectures on psycho-analysis', *Two short accounts of psycho-analysis,* Pelican

Taking notes in lectures 20

We know from studies which have been conducted on note-taking in lectures that deficiencies are due to students' not writing things down, rather than from their writing them down incorrectly, that students need help in selecting what to write down, and that the quality of their notes decreases as the lecture progresses[1]. We also know what teachers can do to help their students to take better notes[2]. For example, they can instruct their students in the skills of taking notes specifically for their own subject material, they can take care to structure their lectures so that note-taking becomes an easier, less chancy affair for students, they can provide cues to indicate when things should be written down, they can ask students for feedback about their lectures, and they can obtain direct feedback by issuing sheets of carbon paper to students and having a look at a copy of their notes.

Even so it is easy for teachers to assume, after a few weeks, that their students have acquired the skills of note-taking only to find, usually by accident, that the notes are woefully deficient. It will set both the teacher's and the students' minds at rest if some time is taken to check up on note-taking. One way of doing this is to use the checklist which follows, or your own variant of it.

References

1   See, for example, Locke E (1977), 'An empirical study of lecture note taking among college students', *Journal of Educational Research*, 71, 93

2   Hartley J & Davis I K (1978), 'Note-taking: a critical review', *Programmed Learning and Educational Technology*, 15, 207-224

How to run the exercise

a   Give students copies of the handouts, 'Exercise: Taking notes in lectures' and 'Checklist': Taking notes in lectures'.

b   Watch the time and tell students when to move on to each new stage of the exercise.

c   When they reach the final stage, encourage them to look for ways of following through their ideas, e.g. by making immediate requests of you or by planning to approach some of their other teachers.

Exercise: Taking notes in lectures

---

a   Complete the checklist, 'Taking notes in lectures'. (4 minutes)

b   Do 'I'll show you mine if you'll show me yours ...' with your neighbour. (4 minutes)

c   Join up with another pair to form a group of four. Go through the list, item by item, together with any extra items that people have written in. Produce a list entitled 'Ways in which my teacher could help me to take better notes'. (15 minutes)

d   Choose a representative from your group to write your list on the board.

e   Discuss how you can use the list which you have produced.

Checklist: Taking notes in lectures

Read the list of statements below and tick those which you feel apply to you. If you wish to comment on any item, or if you feel any important aspects have been omitted, add them in the spaces provided.

1   I find I write very few notes in lectures.   ....

2   My notes seem to contain a number of inaccuracies.   ....

3   I find it hard to take notes consistently throughout lectures.   ....

4   I would like to know how to organise my notes better.   ....

5   I would like to know in advance the way in which the lecture
    is to be organised.   ....

6   My file seems to be one great bundle of paper.   ....

7   I would like more information about the main points of the
    lecture: important names, references etc.   ....

8   Often I don't know whether I need to write something down or not. ....

9   When I'm taking notes I miss a lot of what the lecturer says.   ....

10 Some lecturers don't seem to realise how difficult it is
    to take notes in their lectures.   ....

11 I never look back at my notes.   ....

12 I wish I knew shorthand.

Five teachers 21

Inexperienced students tend to think that they should respond to all lectures in the same way. This is evident in their note-taking, which may be identical in form and method regardless of the type of lecture. But, in fact, teachers are attempting to do very different kinds of things with their lectures, and they have very different expectations of their students as a result. What is sensible for a student to do in one lecture may be quite inappropriate in another. Unfortunately most teachers do not tell their students what they expect of them and students have to learn to work this out for themselves. They have to learn to recognise the real demands of the learning tasks they are faced with.

In the exercise which follows students are helped to recognise the different types of lectures they attend, and to decide how they should go about making the best use of these lectures as a consequence. In particular they are helped to decide what kinds of notes to take.

Although this exercise is set in the context of learning from lectures, students face similar problems in all aspects of their studies. Once they have done this exercise they could attempt a similar analysis of other aspects of their learning such as the varying demands made on them by different kinds of discussion group.

How to run the exercise

(This is written in the form of a script for the teacher who is running the exercise.)

a   'Read the caricatured descriptions of the five different teachers and their lectures. List all your own teachers and then categorise them all in terms of these caricatures. Are they Dr. Torts or Mr. Systems? If the caricatures don't fit your teachers, invent your own caricatures and give them names.' (10 minutes) b   'Describe your teachers to your neighbour, using the five caricatures and any that you have invented. If you have the same teachers, see if you have categorised them in the same way.' (10 minutes)

c   'Form groups of four. Take each of your teachers in turn. Say for each one what you should do in order to learn while sitting in his or her lectures. In particular, what kind of notes would it be sensible for you to take?' (20 minutes)

d   'I'd like each group of four to select a teacher and describe to the class what sort of a teacher he or she is, in terms of the caricatures, and then say what you think it is sensible for a student to do in that teacher's lectures. I'll take one example from each group in turn.' (20 minutes)

e   An open discussion can be developed out of these group reports.

Handout: Five teachers

Dr. Tort expects her students to learn legal principles from books and to apply those principles to specific cases in the seminars. In her law lectures she demonstrates how to apply principles to cases. She is 'modelling' by lecturing, saying 'I want you to be able to do it like this'.

Mr. Spanner gives mechanics lectures as a way of delivering course material to his students. He is expecting them to copy from the board everything that he writes there. He is copying from his notes. His notes are copied from textbooks which are available in the library and in bookshops. His lectures give students selected extracts, with some commentary, from these books.

Dr. Group talks about the sociology of groups in his lectures. The books (and there are twenty on his reading list for each lecture and hundreds in the library) all seem somewhat tangential to the topic. They all use special terminology and are difficult to make sense of. The lecture is a guide to a strange land. Dr Group gives students a map, indicates landmarks to look out for, and points out a few things about this strange land which they might have had trouble finding on their own. He gives them a tourist's smattering of the language they will need in this land. He is trying to prevent them from getting lost when they start reading.

Mr. System tells students the five elements of personnel management in his lecture. Each element has five sub-elements, and he gives an example of each. He is going to test students to see whether they can list these elements and give examples. His lectures are the content of the course. If students take a full set of notes and memorise them, they will pass the course.

93

Dr. Engels tries to explain dialectical materialism in her lecture. It is a difficult idea to grasp. She uses illustrations and metaphors. She repeats herself. She accepts questions from students. She uses every device she can think of to get the concept across. She doesn't care whether students take any notes or not as long as they understand dialectical materialism better than they did before.

Using patterns   22

Most students write notes in linear form. They start at the top of the page and work down, listing headings and subheadings and indenting across the page. An alternative to linear notes is what are known as organic or patterned notes. Patterned notes start in the middle of the page and work outwards along lines of association. These lines are each identified by a single word or phrase, or even a small diagram or other mnemonic. The lines further away from the centre are the equivalent of indented items; they are sub-categories or examples of the lines nearer the centre. Where patterned notes chiefly differ from linear notes is that they allow lines to be drawn and labelled between different parts of the pattern. This enables the creative construction of connections and relationships, and the restructuring of the way a topic is understood. Advocates of patterned notes even argue that their structure more closely matches the way knowledge is represented in the brain.

An example of a pattern is given overleaf.

Patterns can be used for taking notes, recalling information and structuring essays. If you introduce your students to the principle, they will find their own ways of using and developing it.

Pattern illustrating study skills

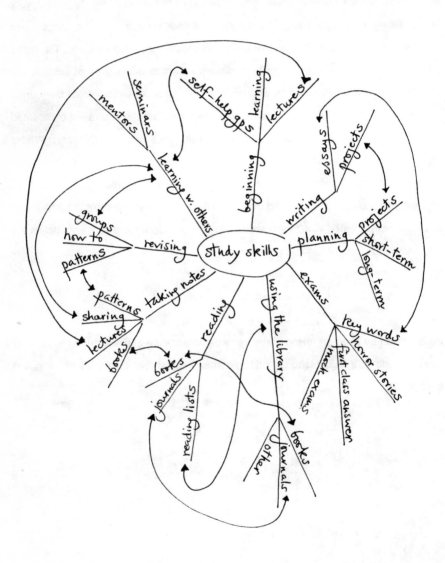

How to run the exercise

a   Suggest that students form pairs.

b   Ask one student in each pair to draw a pattern on a topic you specify, while the
     other student helps by asking the following sorts of question about parts of the
     pattern as they emerge:

     -    'Tell me something about that'

     -    'Tell me something else about that'

     -    'Are there different kinds of that?'

     -    'Can you give me an example of that?'

     -    'Is that related to any of these other things?'

     -    'In what ways are these the same/different?'

c   Ask the students to change roles so that the second student draws a pattern while
     the first student asks the questions. This time the topic for the pattern can be an
     essay title.

d   The students can then have a look at the patterns which have been produced by
     other pairs. They are likely to be much more varied in both structure and content
     than sets of linear notes would be. This variety will give students ideas for adding
     to and modifying their own patterns.

e   Encourage students to continue drawing patterns as part of their studying. You
     could, for example, set them a reading task and ask them to make notes on it in
     the form of patterns which they then bring to the class. Explain to them that once
     they have had experience of the kind of self questioning which is involved, they
     do not need a partner to help them.

Sharing notes

23

There are many occasions when it would be to students' benefit to co-operate with others in the writing of notes. For example:

1   It is difficult to take notes in class as well as participating fully in the discussion. Most students end up with very patchy notes or no notes at all. Students can take it in turns to be the group's note-taker for one class, concentrating on making a full record instead of joining in. These notes should then be written up neatly or typed and a copy made for every group member. At the cost of not joining in one class, students get a full set of notes for the whole series.

2   Some lectures are so fast, or involve such dense new material, that it can be difficult to listen and take notes at the same time. If students try to take full notes then they may either miss bits or fail to understand what they are writing down. Students in pairs can agree to share the task by taking half of the lecture each: one listens and tries to understand; the other takes full notes. Half way through they change roles. Afterwards they swop notes and help each other to understand them. Sharing the demands in this way and swopping over at half time can also make it easier to concentrate for fifty-five minutes.

3   Reference lists which are given to follow up lectures are sometimes long and not very informative. It can be difficult, without going to the library and looking at all the books, to see why they have been listed and whether they seem useful or not. Not many students go to the trouble of checking out every book on the list. Small groups of students can, however, share the task. Each student takes perhaps three references and agrees to find and scan them and to write brief notes about them for the other students in the group, e.g. 'This seems an interesting and very readable text but it only deals with X. There doesn't seem to be anything on Y and as it was published in 1975 there is nothing on Z either. There are three

copies of it, and one in the reserve collection'. Listing the chapter headings and summarising the concluding chapter can also be useful. The students then exchange photocopies of their notes so that they all have information on every book on the list.

How to run the exercise

a   Explain these possibilities to your students and suggest that they form pairs or small groups to consider them and to think up other alternatives.

b   Ask each pair or group to identify at least one shared note-taking activity which they agree to try during the coming week. Encourage them to be specific, e.g. 'Luke and I are each going to take half the notes in the biology lecture at two o'clock on Thursday. And we're going to meet at four o'clock to talk about them'.

c   Ask each pair or group to tell the rest of the class what these agreements are, so that ideas are shared.

d   The following week, spend a few minutes reviewing what happened and, if it worked well, giving the groups time to set up new agreements.

WRITING

How to write an essay

Planning a discussion essay

Explaining

Signposts

Essay writing: diagnostic checklist

Bits of paper

Project pictures

How to write an essay

24

It's not enough just to tell students the principles of essay writing: they need to see how these principles work in practice and to be involved in deciding for themselves what makes a good essay.

How to run the exercise

a   For this exercise you will need a copy for each student of two essays on the same topic, one of which illustrates good essay writing practice and the other which illustrates poor practice. It is better if you obtain these, with permission, from students in a group other than the one doing the exercise.

At the end of the exercise you will also need a copy for each student of an essay writing checklist from a recent study skills handbook.

b   Hand out copies of the two essays and give students the following instructions: 'Read these two essays and decide which one answers the question better. Imagine that you are marking them and write some comments in the margins. Write a general comment at the end. You can give them both a grade if you like. Use a red pen if it helps you to be critical. You have ... minutes for this part of the exercise'. (The time they need will depend on the length and complexity of the essays.)

c   Get the students to form pairs. Ask them to tell each other which essay they thought was better and show each other their comments. (5 minutes)

d   Get pairs to join together to make groups of four. Give the groups these instructions: 'Think about the criteria which your criticisms are based on and in your groups of four list these under the heading "How to write an essay". Choose someone from your group to be spokesperson. You have 10 minutes for this'.

e   Using contributions from the groups, draw up a checklist on the board.

f   Give the students copies of the published checklist so that they can make comparisons, check for omissions and congratulate themselves on having done at least as well as the published author.

Planning a discussion essay

25

Students do not always appreciate the difference between a descriptive essay (e.g. 'The functions of lysosomes' or 'Describe the events leading up to the First World War') and a discussion essay (e.g. 'Lysosomes have been called "suicide bags". Is this an appropriate name?' or 'The First World War was undertaken for economic reasons. Discuss').

Students who know how to write a competent descriptive essay can have difficulty coping with a discussion essay: they can fail to recognise that they must cover both sides of the question, back up their points with facts and discussion and weigh up the evidence in some kind of conclusion.

This exercise takes them step by step through the necessary process.

How to run the exercise

a   Choose an essay question for the group to work with. You can use a course assignment title or invent your own.

b   Take the students through the stages of the planning process overleaf. It is better to present these one by one (you can use the 'gradual reveal' method on the overhead projector) and get students to write their notes on each stage before going on to the next. You can give them a copy of the whole process on a handout at the end.

Handout: A strategy for planning a discussion essay

1   Note points for and points against.

2   Rank the points for and against in order of importance.

3   For each point make brief notes on the facts it will cover and your discussion of them.

4   Decide on an order for your material. Should you deal first with all the 'points for' (in order of importance) and follow this with all the 'points against' or should you alternate your points for and against?

5   Decide on the conclusion.

6   Consider the signposts which will be needed to help a reader to follow your argument. Make it clear whether you are citing evidence, drawing a reasoned conclusion or putting a counter argument. Use such phrases as:
    - This clearly demonstrates that ...
    - It has been argued that ...
    - On the other hand ...
    - However, this conflicts with ...

7   Write a draft introduction.

8   Show your plan to a friend and ask for comments.

Explaining

26

Much of the writing which students have to do involves explaining. The forms in which they are asked to write, however, and especially the essay form, can obscure this apparently obvious point. Writing essays often seems to students to be an odd thing to do. The audience usually consists of a single teacher who knows more than the students about the essay topic. Students can find it difficult to decide how to explain something to someone who already understands what it is they are struggling to explain. Consequently they often assume too much of their reader, and their writing becomes opaque. Logical steps are missed out, and signposts are under-used. Often the reader is not told at the outset where the explanation will lead or even, at the end, what the conclusion is. When so much is taken for granted it can be difficult for the teacher to tell whether or not the student understands the topic.

It is not always very helpful to students to give them general advice about how to write explanations. Instead, in this exercise, students are set the practical task of explaining something with which they are very familiar. From this it is easy to extract general principles about what makes a clear explanation. The group can then discuss how these general principles apply to tasks such as essay writing.

How to run the exercise

a   Divide the class into two groups. Give students copies of the handout, 'Exercise: Explaining'. Ask one group to do task no 1 and the other group to do task no 2.

b   Watch the time and tell students when to move on to each new stage of the exercise.

c   When they reach the listing stage, write their contributions on the board.
    The kinds of device which students tend to choose include:

- making a clear statement of the task ('The station is about three miles to the south and it will take you about half an hour if you go by bus');

- dividing up the task into sections ('I'm going to explain to you how to get out of the building, then how to get to the bus stop, then how to walk from the bus stop at the other end');

- summarising sections when completed ('You will now have completed the bus ride and need to walk the rest of the way').

d   When they reach the discussion stage, encourage them to think seriously about the applications of this exercise to the writing which they do on their course.

Exercise: Explaining

a 1 Write a set of instructions so that a stranger to the area could get to the nearest railway station from this room. Write them as clearly as possible so that the stranger will not get lost or confused.

   2 Write a set of instructions so that someone who has never been in or even seen a kitchen or an egg could safely boil and eat an egg.

   (You have 15 minutes for this.)

b In threes, read each others' instructions. Pick out the clearest bits and put them together into one set of instructions. (10 minutes)

c Get together with one of the groups of three from the other half of the class. Swop your instructions and read them, imagining that you have to follow them. Pick out any problems, things that aren't clear, ambiguous bits, and so on. Tell the three who wrote them which bits are explained well and which bits you would have difficulty with.

d In your group of three, use the comments from the other group of three to rewrite your instructions in an improved form. (5 minutes)

e Pass your sets of instructions round the class so that other groups can read them and see how you wrote them. (5 minutes)

f In your groups of three, choose one good feature of your instructions to tell to the rest of the class. These will be listed on the board.

g Look at the list on the board and try to think of ways in which these principles could be applied to the writing of essays. This is an open discussion.

Signposts

27

It is sometimes the case that students are quite clear in their own minds about what they are doing when writing their essays - what the frame of reference is, how the material is organised, what the main points are etc. - and yet they can fail to make this clear to the reader so that when the essays come back marked they are peppered with such questions as 'So what?' 'What are you getting at?' 'Where is this essay going?' or 'Where does this idea come from?'

This exercise helps students to recognise the importance of saying what they are doing and to find their own ways of signposting the process of their essays.

How to run the exercise

a   Give students copies of the handout and ask them to make notes in the right-hand column. They can also add items to the left-hand column if they wish.

b   Their ideas can then be collated by you on the board or by them in small groups. (Alternatively, with a good group, instead of giving them the handout, you can simply write the two headings on the board and ask students to complete first the left-hand column and then the right.)

c   It is helpful if you follow up this exercise by commenting on signposts or their absence when you mark your students' essays and by asking your colleagues to do the same.

I need to indicate....   **How it could be indicated...**

1   that I understand what the essay question or title is about;

2   the frame of reference I intend to use in my answer;

3   the structure of the essay;

4   the direction I'm taking through the essay as it develops;

5   which are the main points I'm making;

6   the difference between my ideas and other people's;

7   the difference between the views c various authors;

8   the difference between arguments I'm making and examples I give;

9   the connection between what I'm writing and the essay title or question;

10   links between sentences to do with the same point;

11   links between paragraphs in the same section of the essay;

12   how the sections lead to a conclusion or answer;

13   the conclusion I've arrived at.

14

15

Essay writing: diagnostic checklist 28

Before you can start to help your students improve their essay writing, you need to find out what their problems are. One of the best ways of doing this is to ask them. If they are involved in identifying their own needs they will be better motivated to benefit from the help you offer.

How to run the exercise

a   Give your students the checklist and ask them to tick the items which apply to them. (You can of course adapt the list by adding further items to suit your own students.)

b   Find out how many students have ticked each item, either by asking them or by taking in the sheets if the group is very big.

c   You will need to respond to different items in different ways. Some examples follow.

5   'I don't discuss my essay with the teacher before writing it.'

6   'I don't discuss my essay with the teacher after it has been marked.'

Ask students,'Would you like to discuss your essays with your teacher before and/or after writing them?' If they say they would, they will need to be encouraged to explore ways of negotiating this with the people who teach them.

8   'I don't know how to plan an essay.'

You can respond to this by running an exercise on structuring essays **(see 25).**

10 'I often go off the point'

You can respond to this by getting your students to identify ways of helping themselves keep to the point. These can be generated by means of a brainstorm **(see Introduction).**

13 'I'm hoples at speling'

Students who have ticked this item are likely to be in a minority. However, the treatment is quite simple. Suggest that they list in a notebook all the spelling mistakes they have made in their last few essays. (If these have not been picked up by the people who marked the essays the students will need to go back to them and ask them to do this.) The students should then analyse their lists in terms of the type of mistake. For example, if a list contains several mis-spelt adverbs the student concerned can look up the rules for the formation of adverbs in a reference book. Spellings which are idiosyncratic will have to be learned individually. Students can help each other here by working in pairs and testing each other.

They can add to the list in the notebook each time they write an essay though, if they conscientiously learn their spellings, they will make fewer mistakes as time goes on. Because people repeatedly mis-spell the same words, and because students use a limited vocabulary in writing their essays, they will find that correcting the spelling of only a couple of dozen words will have a dramatic effect on their writing.

Checklist: Essay writing

Please tick the statements which apply to you, adding any comments you wish. Two lines have been left blank at the end for you to fill in statements of your own.

1   I don't know what's expected of me when I write an essay.   ....

2   I don't know why I don't get higher grades.   ....

3   I don't see other students' essays.   ....

4   I haven't read an 'A' grade essay on this course.   ....

5   I don't discuss my essay with the teacher before writing it.   ....

6   I don't discuss my essay with the teacher after it has been marked.   ....

7   I don't discuss my essay with other students.   ....

8   I don't know how to plan an essay.   ....

9   I find it difficult to cut my material to the right length.   ....

10   I often go off the point.   ....

11   I don't know the rules of punctuation.   ....

12   People say they can't read my writing.   ....

13   I hoples at speling.   ....

14   _____   ....

15   _____   ....

Bits of paper 29

Some students write poor essays because they don't put enough time and effort into preparing them. Many others, however, read numerous books and produce huge quantities of notes but still fail to do themselves justice because they don't know how to deal with the volume of material which they have generated.

If students come to you in confusion with piles of notes this is an exercise you could run. It probably works best with one student at a time because it requires a lot of space. There are advantages, however, in running it with a group of students: they can compare their results and give one another feedback.

How to run the exercise

a   Ask the student to write down the essay question, together with an 'answer' (however crude) in the form of a few short sentences which summarise what she wants to say on the topic, e.g.

Q   'Population growth: the cause or the consequence of the Industrial Revolution?'

A   *Early census figures indicate that population growth was taking place well before the accepted start of the Industrial Revolution. The increasing pace of industrial development through the late 18th and 19th centuries served only to emphasise a trend that was already happening.*

Q   'What are some of the causes of juvenile delinquency?'

A   *There are plenty of reasons for juvenile delinquency. It's a combination of social, sub-cultural, psychological, economic and political factors, all of which contribute to the present growing incidence of JD.*

b   Ask the student to go through her notes and number each page, section or reference. Then ask her to go through the numbered pieces and write down, on a separate slip of paper for each, one sentence which says what each piece is about.

c   Ask her to place the separate slips of paper on the floor, or on a large table, and to sort them out as far as possible into an order that makes some kind of sense to her, bearing in mind the 'answer' which she identified earlier.

d   As a teacher you are probably quite good at structuring essay material. So you can help her now to identify any obvious gaps in the material and fill them in with slips of paper indicating further arguments, additional data or any other supporting information. It is unlikely that the numbers on these various bits of paper will be consecutive so it is important at this stage to get her to make a note of the resulting sequence of numbers so that it can be replicated later if necessary.

e   Ask her to collect up the bits of paper, shuffle them and repeat the process described in c above, but this time ask her to give the material a different 'shape', e.g.

-    the chronological sequence;

-    the range of points from the most important to the least important;

-    the listing of points for and points against.

After each 'sort' it is important that the sequence of numbers on the bits of paper is recorded for subsequent retrieval if needed.

f   Point out to her that she has shown that she is able to manipulate material and produce an essay of her own design in a sequence that is clear and logical. She began with a series of random notes which she has now fashioned into structured prose.

Project pictures

When students have completed the practical aspects of their projects and are ready to start writing their reports, they usually welcome a study skills session. They need help in giving a shape to the mass of notes, figures and other data which they have accumulated. Even science students, who are used to writing reports, can find projects daunting.

This exercise offers students a simple method of giving a shape to their work and an opportunity to talk through their difficulties and receive helpful feedback.

How to run the exercise

(This is written in the form of a script for the teacher who is running the exercise.)

a   'For this exercise I'd like you to take a piece of paper and draw a diagram or other visual representation of your project. Don't worry about what you know about project reports: just think about the work you've done and the data you've accumulated and put them into some kind of shape on the paper.' (15 minutes)

b   'Now we're going to go round the group and I'd like each of you in turn to hold up your piece of paper and describe what you've drawn. Explain how the bits fit together and tell the rest of us about any insights you've had or problems you've encountered. We'll give you feedback and make suggestions if you want us to.' (about 2 minutes per student)

LEARNING WITH OTHERS

The worst seminar I ever attended

Class contract

Class audit

Mentors

Interacting with others

Checking up on the seminar

Videotaping the group

Student-led seminars

The worst seminar I ever attended 31

Students sometimes seem incapable of making good use of the opportunities offered by seminars to discuss course material in a group and get feedback on their ideas from teachers and fellow students. They don't prepare, they don't join in, they don't ask questions, they don't take notes, they amble off into irrelevancies, and so on. But if you ask students what went wrong in a particular seminar they can usually identify the main problems very readily, including those which are their own responsibility. This exercise makes use of students' own experience and awareness to help them to draw up guidelines and action plans for learning from seminars.

How to run the exercise

(This is written in the form of a script for the teacher who is running the exercise.)

a   'Think back to the worst seminar or group tutorial you have ever had. Note down some of the things which made it bad. Concentrate on things which you or other students did rather than just blaming the teacher. Use the handout to write your notes. [see handout overleaf] You've got 5 minutes for this.'

b   'Now get into pairs and compare notes : describe your experiences to each other and start to draw out things which students can do which make seminars go badly. You've got 10 minutes for this.'

c   'Now join up with another pair to make groups of four. In your groups, draw up a list of things which students do which tend to make discussions go badly and a parallel list of things which make discussions go well. You've got 20 minutes for this.'

d   'Now I'd like each group in turn to read out one item from their list of things which hamper discussions, and one item from their list of things which help. I'll check these out with the other groups and then write them on the board so that we have a full list of everything which we feel affects the usefulness of discussions. You can write the list on your handouts.'

e   'Have a look at the list on the board. Think about a specific seminar coming up soon and choose a couple of things which you are prepared to do (and not do!) to make this a more productive discussion. Write these on your handout. You have five minutes for this.'

f   'Show the other people in your group of four what you have decided to do.'

g   Some time should be put aside at the start of the next class to discuss what happened when students tried to change their behaviour in seminars. Ideally students should get back into their fours and have their handouts in front of them for this discussion.

Handout: The worst seminar I ever attended

1   What made the worst seminar so bad:

2   What students do to make discussions :

BAD   GOOD

3   What I am going to do to make my next seminar better:

4   What I am NOT going to do, in order to make my next seminar better:

Class contract 32

Much of the effort which goes into improving the effectiveness of student learning is aimed at individuals. Some of the factors which affect the individual, however, are determined by the way the whole class operates. For example, class members may regularly arrive late and interrupt lectures, habitually introduce irrelevancies into discussions, keep copies of crucial library books all term, or refuse to share handouts or notes.

This kind of behaviour can have serious effects on learning.

We have found classes willing to discuss such issues, given the opportunity, and able to agree among themselves on a class contract which will maximise learning. We have found that they set themselves very high standards and show themselves able to maintain them.

This exercise is designed to help students to devise contracts. It is followed by an example of an actual class contract which you may like to show to your students to help them fomulate their own.

How to run the exercise

a   Give students copies of the handout, 'Exercise: Class contract'.

b   Watch the time and tell students when to move on to each new stage of the exercise.

c   When they reach the final stage, collate their contributions on the board. Encourage them to move towards a consensus view of the key issues. Show them the sample contract (which follows) if you think this will be helpful.

d   Rephrase the key issues in terms of a 'contract' and obtain the agreement of the class before finalising it.

e   Write the contract on a sheet of paper and pass it round for everyone to sign as a gesture of commitment.

f   Make a copy of the contract for everyone, to serve as a reminder.

g   Remind the class about their contract, or hold a brief discussion about it, every so often. There may need to be minor modifications because aspects of it may be unworkable or not tight enough.

Handout: Sample contract

We all agree

1   not to interfere with each other's learning;

(This means:

- not delaying or interrupting lectures by arriving late;

- not chatting in lectures or being disruptive if we have to leave early;

- keeping an eye on the time when we are working on practical tasks, and completing them efficiently so that we don't keep other people waiting.)

2   to support each other's learning;

(This means:

- picking up handouts etc. for absent friends;

- sharing library books and books we've bought.)

3   not to criticise each other.

(This means:

- no sexist remarks;

- no laughing at misunderstandings or 'silly' questions or answers.)

Signed:

_____   _____

_____   _____

_____   _____

_____   _____

Exercise: Class contract

a   Write down at least three things which other people in the class sometimes do which make it more difficult for you to learn. (2 minutes)

b   Write down at least two things which other people in the class have done which you have found helpful, and two things which you would like other people to do to help you to learn. (3 minutes)

c   In pairs discuss the points which you have noted down. (10 minutes)

d   Join up with another pair to make a group of four. Start drawing up a list of ways in which you would like all the members of the class, including yourselves, to behave in order to maximise everyone's learning. (20 minutes)

e   Choose a representative from your group to read out your group's list. The lists will be collated on the board.

f   The aim of the final part of this exercise is to arrive at a consensus view of the key issues. This will form the basis of our class contract.

Class audit

33

For every topic on your course there is probably somebody in the class who understands it and could explain it to other students if asked. This is especially true for post-experience and post-graduate courses where students frequently have a high level of personal, practical and subject-related expertise. It is also the case that everyone in the class has areas of knowledge and skills which are incomplete and which need developing. An obvious strategy in this situation is to get students to tutor each other.

There are several good reasons for doing this: explaining something to someone else is an excellent way of learning more about it; students are in a good position to understand each other's problems, and can explain things to each other at the right level; students may find it easier to admit to another student that they don't understand something; on post-experience courses it is likely that the students will know more about the applications of theory than do their lecturers.

One way of facilitating this sharing process is to arrange for students to exchange information about their personal strengths and needs at an early stage of the course. In this exercise posters are used as the medium of communication.

How to run the exercise

a   Give each student a sheet of flipchart paper. Ask them to set out their posters as shown.

b   Ask students to fill in the left-hand columns. In the top one they should list their special skills, knowledge and experience. In the lower one they should list their personal, practical and cognitive needs. The posters are then stuck on the wall.

c   Everyone walks round and reads the posters. If they would like to take advantage of what is being offered or offer assistance themselves, they should sign their names in one of the right-hand columns.

d   Those who want help and those who are offering help can then get together. Small groups can usually manage this themselves, and may be able to arrange meetings outside class contact time; with large groups you may have to look at all the sheets yourself, organise study groups around topics and draw up a timetable for these groups. The groups which emerge can, if they prove to be genuinely useful to their members, develop a life of their own. You may then wish to support them as longer term self-help groups **(see 7).**

Poster: Personal audit

Things I can offer others

Who wants help with this?

1. ....

_____

2. ....

_____

3. ....

_____

4. ....

_____

5. ....

_____

Things I need help with

Who can help me?

1. ....

_____

2. ....

_____

3. ....

_____

4. ....

_____

5. ....

_____

Mentors

34

A mentor is someone other than the teacher who provides a student with advice and support. Mentors can be particularly useful for day-release and part-time students and those on placements who have limited access to teachers, but plenty of access to supervisors and others in their workplace. A mentor can be a friend, a relative, a professional colleague or a neighbour. For full-time students mentors are more likely to be students on another course, or students who took the course last year.

It may be helpful to see the kinds of things which students say about their mentors:

'She points out the things that I hadn't noticed.'
'We discuss the exercises and case studies together before I write anything down.'
'I test my ideas out on him by talking them through with him. It helps me to have to explain myself to someone who isn't studying the same subject, and I get another person's views - they are usually rather different from mine.'
'She checks my arithmetic. I use a calculator and she sometimes picks up silly mistakes.'
'Our regular meetings encourage me and mean that I can keep up my momentum.'
'We talk through difficult points together. He asks me questions which make me realise whether I understand what I'm talking about or not.'
'She reads through my written work before I give it in.'
'He comments on the way I go about my work, which I find really useful.'

This exercise helps students to identify the kind of mentor they need so that they can make a sensible choice. It operates on a modest scale. If it is successful, you may like to consider a grander scheme. Brunel University Students' Union, for example, runs an induction weekend for new students which includes the provision of a mentor, and the Tutor for Overseas Students at Bristol Polytechnic runs a pairing scheme in which established UK students are trained in simple communication and counselling skills so that they can act as responsible mentors for new overseas students.

How to run the exercise

a   In the summer term, produce and distribute a leaflet explaining the job of the mentor and invite this year's students to sign on a list of those willing to act as mentors for next year's new arrivals.

b   In the autumn, invite first year students who would like to have a mentor to come to a meeting.

c   At the meeting, distribute the handout 'Choosing and using a mentor' and allow ten minutes or so for students to work through the first three sections, stopping after each section to discuss with their neighbour what they have decided.

d   When students make their choice (in section 3) some of them will choose someone they already know. These students need to be encouraged to approach that person. Others will have chosen to be paired with someone who is already on the course. You can now give them the names of those students who signed on your list in the summer term.

e   Encourage all students to take the handout to their first meeting with their mentor and answer the questions together.

f   Put aside a few minutes of class time occasionally for students to discuss their experience of working with a mentor.

Handout: Choosing and using a mentor

Section 1: **Which of the following activities would you want your mentor to carry out for you?**

Reading my written work	YES / NO
Drawing up a timetable with me	YES / NO
Discussing exercises, essays, reports I have to do	YES / NO
Commenting on how I do my work	YES / NO
Talking over my ideas with me	YES / NO
Listening to my problems	YES / NO
Putting me in touch with other people	YES / NO
Helping me to find facilities (e.g. a word processor)	YES / NO
Checking my written work for accuracy	YES / NO
Encouraging me to keep up with my studying	YES / NO
Listening to me talking about my course	YES / NO
Testing me with questions	YES / NO

Other things I would want a mentor to do:

Section 2: What sort of person do you want as a mentor?

Someone who is an expert in the subject I'm studying	YES / NO
Someone who is warm and sympathetic	YES / NO
Someone who has studied this kind of course before	YES / NO
Someone who is tough and who will keep me at it	YES / NO

What else is important about the sort of mentor you want?

Section 3: Making the choice

In the light of your answers in sections 1 and 2, can you identify someone who you would like to be your mentor? If so, write this person's name below. (You may like to add a second choice in case your first choice is not available.)

1st choice:

2nd choice:

Section 4: Working out the ground rules

a   Questions

1   How often will you meet?

2   Will you meet regularly? If so, when?

3   If you meet irregularly, who will arrange the meetings?

4   How long will meetings last?

5   How are you going to spend the time when you meet?

6   What else do you need to decide about how you will work together?

b   Advice

1   Try to decide in advance what you are going to do next time you meet. Then you can prepare for the meeting.

2   Remember that you can also communicate by phone and in writing.

Interacting with others

35

Many students, even those who are friendly and sociable, isolate themselves when they are studying: they don't discuss their work with other people, they don't ask for help, they don't express their ideas and feelings. Isolation of this kind not only results in students denying themselves support from others; it also impedes their academic progress.

This exercise is based on a questionnaire for students' own use. It is designed to start them thinking about the extent to which they interact with others and ways in which they could reduce their isolation.

How to run the exercise

a   Ask your students to fill in the questionnaire. An introductory rubric is included.

b   Give students some time (about 20 minutes) to discuss their responses in pairs.

c   Invite them to discuss the issues as a class. To get the discussion started, it may be sufficient for you to say, 'OK, where would you like to begin?' Alternatively, you may need to ask such questions as 'What is it that prevents some students interacting with other people?' or 'What are the areas in which you would like to have more interaction with others?' or 'Have any of you some kind of plan for stepping up your interaction?'

Questionnaire: Interacting with others

Some students discuss their studies with other people. (These 'other people' may be lecturers, librarians, other students on the course, other friends or family members.) Some students, on the other hand, tend not to discuss their studies with other people.

This questionnaire is intended to help you to think about which kind of student you are and whether you are satisfied with your interaction with others.

For each question, tick YES, SOMETIMES or NO. If you tick YES or SOMETIMES, indicate who the other people are.

1   Do you discuss your essays with other people?
     YES, USUALLY_____
     SOMETIMES_____
     NO_____

2   Do you read other students' essays?
     YES, USUALLY_____
     SOMETIMES_____
     NO_____

3   When you can't find what you want in the library, do you ask someone?
     YES, USUALLY_____
     SOMETIMES_____
     NO_____

4   When you want clarification or extra information about a lecture, do you ask for it?
     YES, USUALLY_____
     SOMETIMES_____
     NO_____

5   When you read a good book, do you recommend it to other people?
     YES, USUALLY_____
     SOMETIMES_____
     NO_____

6   When you disagree with lecturers' comments and grades on your written work, do
     you say so?
     YES, USUALLY_____
     SOMETIMES_____
     NO_____

7   When you have an idea in class, do you express it?
     YES, USUALLY_____
     SOMETIMES_____
     NO_____

8   When you feel worried about your work or fed up with the course, do you express
     your feelings?
     YES, USUALLY_____
     SOMETIMES_____
     NO_____

9   When other students annoy you, do you express your annoyance?
     YES, USUALLY_____
     SOMETIMES_____
     NO_____

10   When something on the course interests you, do you show your interest?
     YES, USUALLY_____
     SOMETIMES_____
     NO_____

Checking up on the seminar

36

Sometimes things go wrong in seminar groups. The problem may reveal itself in awkward silences, absenteeism or even arguments. This is clearly a case for treatment. Even groups which are apparently working well, however, can benefit from spending some time looking at their shortcomings and building on their strengths. It is in the interests of both teachers and students for groups to check up from time to time on how their seminars are working.

What you can do

1   A simple way of checking up on the seminar is to use a round. You could say, 'I'd just like to check on how you're all getting along in this seminar group. Let's take it in turns to say "One thing I like about this group and one way in which it could be better for me". I'll join in too. Who'd like to start?'

2   If you suspect that there is a serious problem with the group which needs more thought, you may like to check this out by using a pencil and paper activity. You could say, 'I'm going to ask you to write down some answers to the questions you will see on the OHP screen. Take a couple of minutes to think about each one, and write down your responses on a piece of scrap paper'.

Using an OHP transparency you have prepared beforehand, reveal the following five questions one at a time, allowing time for students to write their answers.

a   **What's going wrong in this group?**

-

-

b   **What could the teacher do about it?**

-

-

c **What could I do about it?**

-

-

d **What's going right in this group?**

-

-

e **What could we do as a group to make it better?**

-

-

Next you can ask students to share their notes with someone else, and then form fours to concentrate on identifying any difficulties they notice in the group and ways of dealing with them.

3 Another pencil and paper activity which can help to identify problems in groups is the checklist. The example which follows was designed specifically for sociology seminars based on prior reading, but could easily be adapted to suit other discipline areas and other types of seminar.

How to run the exercise

(This exercise is particularly effective if it is used after two or three weeks of seminars when people are beginning to feel at ease with each other.)

a You could say, 'The purpose of this activity is to help you to get the most you can out of these seminars and to make them into enjoyable learning experiences. Please read the statements on the checklist and tick the ones which apply to you'.

b After three minutes say, 'Now please turn to your neighbour and have a look at each other's sheets. You've got two minutes to see what the other person has written'.

c   After two minutes say, 'Now I'd like you to form fours. I'd like you to take about twenty minutes to go through the sheet item by item. If any members of your group of four have ticked an item, ask them to explore it for a while and, where possible, those of you who have met, and dealt with, that particular problem can try to find ways of helping them. Remember, the purpose of this exercise is to make these seminars work for us'.

Checklist: Learning in seminars

Read the list of statements below and tick those which you feel apply to you. If you wish to add a comment about any item please use the space provided. If you feel any aspects have been omitted, please add them below.

1   I'm not clear how the seminars relate to other parts of the course.   ......

2   I'm not sure what I'm supposed to do to prepare myself for the seminar.   ......

3   I find it hard to follow the discussion.   ......

4   I find it difficult to ask someone else in the group what's going on.   ......

5   I wouldn't want to explain things to other group members
    because I might be wrong.   ......

6   I'm never sure what to write down during the seminar.   ......

7   I never feel responsible for the success or failure of the seminar.   ......

8   I feel I can't argue with great thinkers and writers.   ......

9   I hardly ever say anything in seminars.   ......

10   _____   ......

11   _____   ......

Videotaping the group

37

One way in which members of a student group can get feedback on their behaviour is to watch a recording of themselves in action. This not only gives them an external view of their own roles in the group but also enables them to judge the dynamics of the whole class from a new perspective.

If, in addition, they are given criteria on which to base their judgements this will help them to identify, and be ready to tackle, those problems which inhibit the effectiveness of the group.

This exercise can be completed in one hour. You can run it in the second part of a two-hour session or, in the case of a one-hour session, in the week following the recording.

How to run the exercise

a   Videotape one of your sessions. A modern portable camera with a wide-angle lens and a built-in microphone should be adequate for this exercise, but take the advice of your audio-visual technician if you aren't sure, or if your early results aren't good enough. You will find that many of the problems which arise from lack of familiarity with the equipment, or the 'cosmetic effect' on group members of having the camera in the room, will disappear after the first few minutes.

b   Before replaying the videotape, ask students to take five minutes to write down what they think the objectives of the session were, and also a few sentences describing their own participation in the group.

(This will give them the opportunity of comparing their subjective view with the videotape.)

c Give students copies of the handout, 'Looking at the group'.

d Divide the class into three groups and ask each group to rate the session in one of the ways listed in section 1 of the handout.

e Replay the videotape, or part of it. (Ten minutes can be enough.)

f Ask each of the subgroups to report on their findings.

g Get students to form pairs to work out their action plans.

h Remember to allow enough time at the end of the next session for 'reporting back'.

Handout: Looking at the group

1   Analysis

As you watch the video, rate the session in one of the following ways:

a   Write down the name of each person who speaks in order of speaking.

b   Note any explicit or implicit statement of objectives.

c   Note any interesting body language (e.g. posture, gesture, facial expression).

2   Reports   (3 x 5 minutes)

Give a report on your analysis and describe examples of helpful and unhelpful behaviour which you noticed.

_____

_____

_____

_____

3   Action Plans (10 minutes)

a   In pairs, identify a task for yourselves which should improve the next session, e.g. 'I will speak in the first five minutes', 'I will invite another student to speak' etc.

_____

_____

_____

b   At the end of the next session, report back to your partner and describe how successful you were.

Student-led seminars 38

Running a seminar is a frightening experience for most students. They find it hard to take responsibility for helping their fellow students to learn and too often they fall back into the old seminar routine of reading out a paper while the rest of the students sit in silence. Teachers can help students to run seminars by explaining exactly what is expected of them and suggesting ways of structuring the session so that it is an enjoyable learning experience for the group. They can encourage them to find ways of involving the other students so that everyone participates and takes advantage of the potential of the group for development and mutual support.

This exercise offers students ideas for running seminars creatively.

How to run the exercise

a   Give students copies of the handout, 'Guidelines for students running seminars', explaining that this is a statement of what they will be expected to do when it's their turn to run the seminar.

b   Take them through the handout, explaining terms such as 'rounds', 'pyramidding' etc. **(See Introduction)** Also tell them what your role will be when a student leads the seminar.

c   Ask them whether these are guidelines which they feel they can work with.

d   Follow this up by being available for discussion with students before and after their seminars.

Handout: Guidelines for students running seminars

A   At the beginning of the seminar

1   Set the tone of the meeting by the content and manner of your introduction.

2   State the objectives of the discussion and, where appropriate, make links with previous and future work.

3   Inform the group briefly of the process to be followed in this seminar with regard to aspects such as timing, the pattern of the session and opportunities for comment, discussion, questions etc.

B   During the seminar

1   Use rounds to obtain the views of all group members, e.g.

-   One thing I learned last week was.....

-   One thing I'm not clear about is.....

-   One question I'd like to ask is.....

2   Use pyramidding to encourage group members to work together.

3   Keep strictly to time in each part of the process.

4   Keep the objectives of the session in front of the group in some way, e.g. verbally, by using the OHP, by using a handout or flipchart.

5   Provide space in the plan for interesting and relevant anecdotes, examples, practical applications, new developments etc.

6   Encourage a balanced discussion or debate by eliciting views from both sides of the argument.

7   Encourage 'low contributors' e.g. by giving them time, preparing questions with them in mind, praising them etc.

8   Praise 'high contributors' when they clarify, summarise or build on the views of

others and when they ask open questions.

9   Remember there may be times when silence is appropriate in the group.

C   At the end of the seminar

1   Identify which objectives of the session have been achieved and which remain to be dealt with outside the group by private study, private discussion, further reading, assignments etc.

2   Agree and note any conclusions which can be drawn from the discussion.

3   If possible, provide people with a few minutes to make notes for themselves about the seminar.

USING THE LIBRARY

Library quiz

Paper-chase

Without reading the book

This is how it works

Library quiz

39

Students are often taken on a tour of the library as part of their introduction to college. Such a tour can be helpful in familiarising them with the layout of the library, introducing them to library staff and giving them a sense of the variety of resources available. But it needs to be followed up with an activity which helps them to be efficient users of the library.

This exercise was written by Joyce Davies, Humanities Librarian at Bristol Polytechnic, for literature students studying *Macbeth*. It illustrates the type of exercise which requires students to explore and work with the resources of the library. Normally the questions would be spaced out so that students could write their answers on the sheet, but here we have simply listed the questions to demonstrate the method. Notice that the questions are not only based in the students' own discipline but are restricted to a limited topic area within that discipline so as to illustrate the differences between the various reference sources.

How to run the exercise

a   Work closely with a subject specialist librarian if possible.

b   You will need to design your own exercises to suit your own subject area and to take account of the way in which resources in your subject are organised in your library. Try to think of the kinds of information you want your students to be able to find, the techniques they will need to use to find them, and the kinds of problem they are likely to encounter. Always test out your exercises by doing them yourself first.

c   Give students copies of the exercise and ask them to note down the answers to the questions. Encourage them to ask for help if they get stuck.

d   Arrange a classroom discussion immediately after the library activity so that students can present problems and discuss more general library issues with you and the subject librarian.

Author catalogue

1   How many copies of Shakespeare's *Macbeth* does the library have?

2   Does it have the Arden edition?

3   Does the library have any criticisms of *Macbeth*?

4   Find the class number for John Wain's *Macbeth*, in the Casebook Series.

Subject index and classified catalogue

1   Find the class number for concordances of Shakespeare's work.

2   What class number is used for poems by Shakespeare?

3   How many books does the library have at this number?

Bibliographies

1   Using B.N.B. for 1980, find the class number for books on Macbeth, King of Scotland.

2   How would you find the publisher of a book called *Twentieth Century Interpretations of Macbeth*, published in 1977? Is it still in print?

3   Does the library have a bibliography which would list articles about the Polanski film of *Macbeth*?

4   Locate *The Year's Work in English Studies*. How does it differ from a bibliography of abstracts and indexes?

Reference

1   Where would you find a brief biography of William Shakespeare?

2   Where would you find a short synopsis of Shakespeare's *Macbeth* ?

3   Where would you find a biography of Macbeth?

4   What do the following mean?

ibid.

et al.

inter alia

c.f.

i.e.

5   Where would you find a list of the kings and queens of Scotland following Macbeth?

Periodicals

1   Is the periodical *Drama Review* held in any of the college libraries?

2   Where would you find the back numbers of *Literature and History* in this library?

3   In 1973 a book called *Shakespeare's Talking Animals* by Terence Hawkes was published. Did the *Critical Quarterly* review it?

Abstracts and indexes

1   Were any periodical articles written on the Shakespeare Memorial Theatre, Stratford-upon-Avon, in 1979?

2   How many periodical articles were written on William Shakespeare in 1982? How many were about *Macbeth*?

3   What are the differences between the entries in *British Humanities Index* and *Historical Abstracts*?

4   What information would you expect to find in a bibliographical entry for a journal article?

Paper-chase

40

This exercise is based on guidelines devised by Jo Corke, Bristol Polytechnic, to introduce first year biology students to scientific journals. While it is specific to the needs of a particular group of students, it also demonstrates a method which can be adapted and used to familiarise students in other disciplines with the conventions of journals. It would not be difficult to produce a similar exercise to this using sociological, historical or computing journals.

You may want to use this type of exercise not only to develop students' study skills, but also as a means of teaching a particular topic. If the exercise is given a single theme, such as (with science students) nitrogen fixation, or different practical techniques, it can become part of a structured approach to independent learning.

How to run the exercise

a You will need to devise your own exercise to illustrate the characteristics of journals in your own subject area. You may be able to obtain help from a specialist subject librarian. Always test out an exercise by doing it yourself first.

b Choose a time for the exercise when your subject librarian is available to help you.

c Give students copies of the exercise and ask them to note down the answers to the questions. Encourage them to ask for help if they get stuck.

d Arrange a classroom discussion immediately after the library activity so that students can present problems and discuss more general library issues with you and the subject librarian.

Work through the handout. You will need a note-pad to jot down answers. Also note down any comments or questions which you may want to bring up in the discussion later.

a   Find *The Journal of Applied Bacteriology.* What publications are on the shelf either side of this journal? What does this tell you about the system of placing journals in the library?

b   Would you expect to find *The Biochemical Journal* before or after *The Journal of Applied Bacteriology*? Find this journal; does this confirm or alter your ideas about journal organisation in the library?

c   Choose one issue (or bound volume) of *The Journal of Applied Bacteriology* and find the list of contents. The titles of the articles are designed to be sufficiently detailed to give you an immediate idea of the subject matter. Look for key words such as

- the names of specific organisms, e.g. 'The incidence of *Salmonella* in animal feeds';

- the names of specific products, e.g. 'The long-term effect of kerosine pollution on the microflora of moorland soils';

- the names of specific microbial activities, e.g. 'The development of the anaerobic spoilage flora of meat stored at chill temperatures'.

From the issue you have selected, find three articles with titles demonstrating key words of each of the three types listed above and write a reference for each of these using the journal's own format.

d   Answer the following questions about the organism named in one of your chosen references. (Use the summary of the article, the introduction or your microbiology textbook to help you.)

-   Is the organism under investigation an alga, fungus, bacterium or virus? Is your answer expected in view of the title of the journal?

-   If it is a bacterium find out a few taxonomic details, e.g. gram reaction, sporing ability, shape, habitat.

-   What particular aspect of the microbe's existence is being investigated?

e   Look up the reference list at the end of any paper in *The Biochemical Journal* and find a reference to a book. Cite a reference to a chapter of your microbiology textbook to the format used by *The Biochemical Journal*.

f   Write down the abbreviated titles of *The Journal of Applied Biology* and *The Journal of Biochemistry*, as used by the two journals. Compare their reference lists. Do they use the same abbreviations for all journal titles?

Without reading the book 41

Students frequently find that the book which they have been recommended to read is not in the library. This can be enough to make them abandon all attempts to study that topic.

A variety of factors contribute to the difficulty which students experience in gaining access to written sources. Student poverty, the persistent reduction in library budgets and heavy demands on books due to large class sizes are just a few of the more obvious factors which are outside the control of even the most determined learner.

What students can do is find alternatives to the recommended text. There are usually plenty of these, though they are not always obvious or easy to locate. Simply telling students about alternatives may not be very helpful; they need to try them out for themselves.

How to run the exercise

a   Choose several different books, of which the library holds only one copy. Borrow these and take them to the class.

b   Say to the students 'I recommend that you read these books. Unfortunately these are the only copies and you can't borrow them from me. What I want you to do is to form pairs and go to the library now and find alternatives to these books. Come back in half an hour and we'll discuss what you have discovered about what you can do when the book you want is out'.

c   When the students come back, go round each pair in turn asking them to describe one method or source which they found useful. List these on the board. Keep picking up ideas and adding them to the list until no new ones emerge.

Add other alternatives only if students do not discover these for themselves.

d   Write up this list as a handout and copy it for the class to use next time the book they want is out. The list should include:

- other books by the same author;

- journal articles by the same author;

- jointly authored books;

- contributions by the author to collections of articles or books of 'readings' edited by others;

- other books on the same topic by different authors, particularly more recent textbooks which might refer back to the one which was recommended;

- an earlier edition of the book;

- reviews;

- radio and television programmes which are scripted or introduced by the authors or deal with the set topic;

- Open University units, texts, radio and television programmes on the set topic;

- encyclopedias;

- dictionaries specialising in the set subject;

- subject-based periodicals;

- magazines.

This is how it works

Modern libraries increasingly contain a wide range of sophisticated electronic equipment with which their materials may be accessed. Some of this equipment, such as videotape recorders and micro-computers, will be familiar to users since it is in everyday use in many households.

It remains the case, however, that many students will be deterred from using the available resources due to a lack of confidence in handling the equipment. One reason for this is that there are, for example, several types of videotape recorder, tape-slide replay equipment, and personal computer, each of which has a different operating system; the ability to use one of them does not automatically imply the ability to use all of them. One way of dealing with this problem in a non-threatening and time-saving way is to identify the equipment by type and then to get students to teach each other how to use it.

How to run the exercise

a   Make a handout as follows: list all the types of equipment in your library; for each piece of equipment devise an information question which will test its use; leave space for students to sign their names to show whether or not they know how to use the pieces of equipment. An example of one such handout follows.

b   Pair students off as 'teacher' and 'learner' and send them to the library. The job of the 'teachers' is to demonstrate how to use the equipment; the task for the 'learners' is to show that they can access the answers to the questions on the handout. Students will need to change roles and also change partners until they are all familiar with all the equipment.

c   At the end of the session deal with any difficulties which remain.

Handout: Library equipment

Equipment & Question	I can demonstrate this	I would like to be shown how to use this

**MICROFILM READER
(Bell & Howell MR31)**

What was the topic of
the leader article of *The
Times* on 15.03.1940?
Answer:

**VIDEO PLAYBACK
(VHS)**

Run TV programme 1 of
the OU's D102 Course.
Who is the presenter?
Answer:

**TAPE SLIDE
(Caramate)**

What journal is featured
in unit 3 of the series
Microbiological Abstracts?
Answer:

**MICROFICHE READER
(Fuji)**

In the *Torts* pack,
which case is referred to
on Fiche no 5, Frame 22?
Answer:

REVISING

Revising right, revising wrong

How my teachers could help me

What's your worry?

Using patterns in revision

Group preparation for exams

Action plans

Any questions?

Revising right, revising wrong 43

There is no one correct way to revise; different methods suit different individuals. You can help your students not by telling them how to revise but by encouraging them to make their own selection from a range of suggestions. And the more these suggestions are based on hard won experience rather than theory, the more likely students are to want to try them out.

This exercise helps the group to reflect on their own revision strategies and to generate plenty of ideas from which to choose.

How to run the exercise

a   Ask students in turn to describe one thing they do when they revise efficiently and one thing they do when they revise inefficiently. (The kind of thing they will say will be 'When I'm revising right, I'm thinking of questions to test myself and when I'm revising wrong, I'm staring at my notes and thinking about something else' or 'When I'm revising right, I'm working at things in a logical order and when I'm revising wrong, I'm reading stuff I already know and postponing the stuff I'm worried about'.)

b   Encourage other members of the group to ask questions, make comments and in particular to press for details about methods which they are thinking of trying.

c   Ask students to write down the details of at least one method which they intend to try and to specify the material they plan to use it on. (e.g. 'I'm going to start my ecology revision by making a list of past questions on ecosystems and then I'll look for the answers to the questions in my notes.') If you give them three minutes each in pairs to tell their partners what they plan to do, this will help them to clarify it.

How my teachers could help me 44

Decisions about what will happen in revision sessions are usually made by the teachers. Since these decisions are based on the teachers' assumptions about the students, it is unlikely that they will reflect exactly what the students want. If, on the other hand, students are asked to specify how their teachers can help them, revision sessions can be structured as a response to their needs.

This exercise is based on the assumptions that students are in the best position to know what their learning needs are and that they are able and willing to specify these needs given a little encouragement.

How to run the exercise

a   Ask your students to do a five-minute brainstorm on 'Ways in which my teachers could help me to revise'. When using this technique, it is important not to respond to their suggestions while the brainstorm is in progress. **(See Introduction)**

b   Get the students to sort out the list of brainstorm items. For example, at this stage they may want to cut out the jokes ('My teacher could sit the exam for me'), specify some items more clearly ('Revision seminars: *we could give the teacher a list of topics the week before*') and group items according to different teachers.

c   Ask students which items apply to *you* and negotiate there and then what you will do to help. Make sure that this agreement is specific enough for students to be sure that they are getting the help they want. For example, 'I will bring spare copies of the syllabus to the next seminar and we will spend ten minutes identifying the major topics on this year's course. Then I'll give you two sample exam questions to illustrate each topic'.

d   Encourage students to negotiate similar agreements with other teachers.

What's your worry?

The revision period is a very stressful time for students. Many of them are so anxious about the exams that they find it difficult to concentrate on preparing for them. And in addition the competitive nature of the education system leads them to believe that they must not express their anxieties but remain isolated in strained misery until it's all over.

This exercise challenges such secrecy and encourages students to talk about their anxieties, give one another support and develop a more positive attitude to the exams.

The exercise is based on a checklist of common student anxieties. An example of a checklist follows; you may, however, wish to devise a new one to fit your own situation or ask your students to produce their own by means of a quick brainstorm **(see Introduction)** at the start of the session.

How to run the exercise

a   Hand round copies of 'Checklist: Preparing for exams' and ask students to spend a few minutes completing it. Reassure them that if they want to tick all the items, that's all right.

b   Ask students to form pairs and talk to each other for a couple of minutes each about the items they have ticked.

c   Ask pairs to join together to make groups of four. Give them the following instructions:

'Go through the list, spending a few minutes on each item. Anyone in your group who has ticked an item can say something about it. Anyone who hasn't ticked the item can offer help to those who have. Choose one member of your group who will write down conclusions, decisions, good ideas or questions to present to the rest of the class at the end'.

d   Ask the spokesperson from each group in turn to give a brief report on one or two helpful points which came out of the group's discussion.

Checklist: Preparing for exams

Read the list of statements below and tick those which you feel apply to you.
If you wish to add a comment about any item, or if you feel any aspects have been omitted, please add them at the end.

1   I find it difficult to begin revision while we are still doing new stuff
     on the course.   .....

2   I sleep badly the night before an exam.   .....

3   I'm always certain I'm going to fail exams.   .....

4   I can't draw up a realistic revision timetable.   .....

5   I can't concentrate on my revision for long enough at a time.   .....

6   I forget things so easily.   .....

7   Other people seem so confident.   .....

8   I can't get down to revision until the last minute.   .....

9   I don't think I work hard enough.   .....

10   Sometimes I feel like giving up.   .....

11   _____   .....

12   _____   .....

Using patterns in revision 46

(This item follows on from **item 22, Using patterns**: students need to be shown how to write patterned notes before they can use them in revision.)

If students organise their revision material in patterns, they can give it a coherent and logical shape and make connections which would be missed in linear notes. A pattern also reveals where there are gaps in the material where further reading and studying need to be done. And it is more memorable because it makes a visual impact.

Once an adequate pattern has been built up, the student can practise reproducing it from memory. This is not the same as the rote learning task of writing out linear notes over and over again, however: each time a pattern is drawn it can be constructed in a different order and built into a different shape, and is likely to develop and change as the topic becomes clearer and more coherent in the student's mind.

Once the pattern has been rewritten a couple of times during revision it becomes easy for the student to draw a version of it quickly during the exam. Any key word in the exam question which is part of the pattern can be used as a starting point. The pattern can then serve as an essay plan.

How to run the exercise

a Set your students exam-type questions in class and ask them to use patterns to recall what they know about the topic and to plan answers. They need not write out the answers as it is in the preparation stage that the pattern is used.

b Gradually reduce the amount of time you allow them to draw the pattern until they are able to produce one in five minutes. (This is probably a realistic estimate of how long a student would spend planning an answer under exam conditions.)

Group preparation for exams

47

Since isolation is one of the main causes of stress during the exam period, students need to be urged to organise themselves into revision groups so that they can not only review the course, ask questions and exchange ideas but also give one another support and encouragement.

One of the polytechnics has produced a glossy study skills guide for its students, with four pages full of advice on exam techniques but no mention at all of any form of group preparation. If groupwork is an effective method of learning in higher education, ways must be sought to make the most of its potential at exam time.

What you can do

1   Tell students about the benefits of revising in groups and encourage them to exchange addresses and telephone numbers.

2   Give students copies of the handout, 'Group preparation for exams', and discuss it with them. **(See also 7 Self-help groups)**

Handout: Group preparation for exams

Group preparation for exams is likely to work better if ...

1   the group comprises a small number of helpful people who already have some sort of positive current relationship, e.g. classmates, friends, parents or relatives;

2   the dates of the meetings are arranged well in advance and the meetings start and stop at agreed times;

3   some sort of programme is planned, e.g. short talks or question and answer sessions based on agreed topics;

4   members check regularly for feelings of competition, resentment or anxiety within the group and encourage positive outcomes to group sessions;

5   meetings are tailored to meet specific exam circumstances, e.g. predictable exam questions or seen exams.

Action plans

48

The lack of an action plan can mean that students postpone their exam revision while there still seems to be plenty of time and then, when the pressure is on, find themselves immobilised by panic.

This exercise encourages them to face the difficulties which lie ahead, to make a realistic assessment of their situation and to pace their work sensibly. (The notions of action plans and helping and hindering factors are taken from life skills training.)

How to run the exercise

(This is written in the form of a script for the teacher who is running the exercise.)

a   'Make a list of all the subjects, options or modules which you are going to be examined in.' (2 minutes)

b   'For each one, note down what *kind* of revision you want to do and where you will start. In other words, how will you spend the first fifteen minutes of the revision time?' (10 minutes)

c   'There are x days between now and the start of the exams. Estimate how many of these days you can use, in whole or in part, as revision days.' (5 minutes)

d   'Using the notes you have made, work out an action plan for yourself.' (5 minutes)

e   'Consider factors which will affect you in carrying out this action plan. Make two separate lists, one of helping factors, such as membership of a revision group or enthusiasm for the course, and the other of hindering factors, such as noisy accommodation or a propensity to panic.' (5 minutes)

f   'Now, in pairs, you have ten minutes each to talk about what you've written and look for ways of boosting the helping factors and reducing the hindering factors.' (20 minutes)

Any questions?   49

When teachers in a revision session give their students the opportunity to ask questions, they and the students generally assume that the only legitimate focus for these questions is the course content. In fact, students usually have plenty of un-answered questions about the marking process in particular and the assessment system in general. They would like to know, for example, how marks are allocated between questions, whether papers are second-marked, when the results are published, what happens to students who fail or fall ill, how the appeals procedure operates etc. If they are given the chance to ask these questions and receive full answers, this will help to alleviate their anxiety about the exams.

What you can do

Set aside some time at the start of a revision session for students to ask questions about the exams. Remember that many aspects of the exam procedure which are obvious to you seem to the students to be mysterious and frightening, so try to answer their questions fully and patiently.

EXAMS

Horror stories

Mock exam

Key words in exam questions

First class answer

Horror stories

It is very easy for students to make mistakes in exams, even when they are well prepared. They may turn up on the wrong day or at the wrong time, answer too many or too few questions, allocate their time unwisely, or miss questions on the back of the exam paper.

Because they find exams so stressful they may respond to bad experiences of this kind by trying to forget them. This exercise gives them an opportunity instead to reflect on their mistakes and learn from them. They can also learn from other people's mistakes.

The exercise needs very little introduction: students quickly see the point of it and normally have no difficulty thinking of incidents to describe.

How to run the exercise

a   Ask members of the group in turn to recount an exam horror story and then to suggest how the mistake could have been avoided. The incident is preferably something which students have experienced though it can be something which they have been told about.

b   If any students have trouble deciding how the mistake could have been avoided, other members of the group can be invited to make suggestions.

c   This exercise gives rise to a lot of laughter as students relive their own experiences and visualise each other's. This laughter should be encouraged as it helps students to express their feelings and serves to release some of the tension that is often around the topic of exams.

Mock exam 51

It is usual for people to put in some practice when they know they are going to be asked to perform. This is true for football matches, driving tests, O and A levels etc. but often does not apply to exams in further and higher education: for many students, the only practice they get is in the exams themselves. Mock exams give students a chance to make their mistakes in a safe situation and learn from them with support from their teachers.

How to run the exercise

a   Your students will need reassurance because even mock exams can be frightening. Explain to them how they will benefit from putting in some practice.

b   Make the exam as realistic as possible: arrange the furniture in formal rows, use a real question paper (from a previous year), maintain complete silence and keep strict time. (You can even write 'Exam began ...' and 'Exam ends ...' on the board.)

c   It is important that the scripts are marked and the students given feedback. If the exam is in a subject which you are not qualified to assess, the students will need to negotiate the marking with their teachers.

Key words in exam questions   52

When acting in their role as examiners, teachers have a special language which students need to learn in order to be able to understand the questions on their exam papers. For example, the instruction to *discuss* is asking students to do something quite different from the instruction to *describe*. If students don't appreciate this difference, they will answer the question inappropriately.

This exercise gives students the opportunity to consider the meanings of such terms, as used by their teachers.

How to run the exercise

a   Make a list of words such as *discuss* , *describe, evaluate, assess* etc. which are used in exam questions. If you take these from past papers, rather than inventing your own list, you can ensure that these are terms which are used by the people who teach your students.

b   Ask your students to clarify the meanings of the words and to differentiate between similar terms. If the group is small, you can run this as an informal discussion, though it is helpful if you write the agreed definitions on the board; in a larger group, students will participate better if they discuss the list in pairs before pooling their ideas with the rest of the class.

c   If there is any doubt in the group about the meaning which their teachers may give to particular terms, you will need to check this out with the teacher concerned and report back to the group the following week.

First class answer 53

Very poor answers on exam scripts give the impression that the candidate was following a set of instructions such as:

'Write down whatever you can think of about this topic, in the order in which you remember things. Do not structure your answer. Include irrelevant material if you can't think of anything better. Abandon all intellectual rigour. Draw no conclusions.'

It is possible to rewrite an exam question in the form in which students with different quality answers appear to have understood it. This exercise gives students the opportunity to try this so that they can compare the different approaches and learn how best to attack exam questions. It was devised by Vicky Lewis, Warwick University.

How to run the exercise

a   Give students copies of 'Handout: First class answer' and a question from last year's exam paper. Ask them to rewrite the question in the same way as the one on the handout. Get them to try on their own for five minutes and then work in groups of three for another five minutes to produce a joint version.

b   Ask the groups of three to read out their versions. If possible, read them one of your own based on what actually happened last year.

c   If students find this either very difficult or very enjoyable, you can run through the process again with a second question.

Exam question

This is a question from a paper on the psychology of child development.

'Compare and contrast the consequences of blindness and deafness for language development.'

This is how students who gained different degree classifications seem to have interpreted the question.

1st Class

'Identify the consequences of blindness and deafness for language development. Compare and contrast these consequences, drawing conclusions about the nature of language development. Comment on the adequacy of theories of language development in the light of your conclusions.'

Upper 2nd Class

'Identify the consequences of blindness and deafness for language development. Compare and contrast these consequences.'

Lower 2nd Class

'List some of the features of blindness and deafness. List some consequences for development including a few for language development.'

3rd Class

'Write down almost anything you can think of about blindness, deafness, child development and language development. Do not draw any justified conclusions.'

TECHNICAL AND EDUCATIONAL SERVICES

INTERESTING WAYS TO TEACH

No 1.	**53 Interesting Things to Do in Your Lectures**	(Revised 1986)
No 2.	**53 Interesting Things to Do in Your Seminars and Tutorials**	(Revised 1987)
No 3.	**53 Interesting Ways to Assess Your Students**	(1986)
No 4.	**53 Interesting Ways of Helping Your Students to Study**	(Summer 1987)
No 5.	**53 Interesting Communication Exercises for Science Students**	(Summer 1987)
No 6.	**53 Interesting Ways to Appraise Your Teaching**	(Summer 1987)

ORDER FORM

Please supply :

<u>No. of copies</u> <u>Total cost</u>

53 Interesting Things to Do in Your Lectures (£6 UK, £9 airmail)

53 Interesting Things to Do in Your Seminars and Tutorials (£6 UK, £9 airmail)

53 Interesting Ways to Assess Your Students (£6 UK, £9 airmail)

53 Interesting Communication Exercises for Science Students (£7 UK, £10 airmail)

53 Interesting Ways of Helping Your Students to Study (£7 UK, £10 airmail)

53 Interesting Ways to Appraise Your Teaching (£6 UK, £9 airmail)

Total   £

Book prices (July 1987) are stated above (inc p&p.) for U.K. and overseas surface mail. Books are sent airmail by specific request at a charge of £3 sterling. A banker's commission of £3.50 should be added to invoices to be settled in currencies other than £ sterling. Discount 10% on 10 or more books.

All orders and invoices to
Technical and Educational Services Ltd, 37 Ravenswood Road, Bristol BS6 6BW U.K.
Ansaphone (0272) 45446.

Please make cheques payable to **'Technical and Educational Services Ltd'.**

Technical and Educational Services Ltd reserve the right to change book prices without notice.

Name

....

Address ....

....

INTERESTING WAYS TO TEACH

No 1. **53 INTERESTING THINGS TO DO IN YOUR LECTURES**

Graham Gibbs Sue Habeshaw Trevor Habeshaw

53 practical ideas in 8 Chapters:

Structuring The Process

Using Handouts

Structuring And Summarising Content

Active Learning During Lectures

Improving Students' Notes

Linking Lectures

Holding Attention

Checking On Learning

No 2. **53 INTERESTING THINGS TO DO IN YOUR SEMINARS AND TUTORIALS**

Sue Habeshaw Trevor Habeshaw Graham Gibbs

53 practical ideas in 8 Chapters :

Starting Off

Encouraging Students To Participate

Encouraging Students To Take Responsibility

Evaluating The Work Of The Group

Student-Led Seminars

Group Work

Written Material

Expressing Feelings

No 3 **53 INTERESTING WAYS TO ASSESS YOUR STUDENTS**

Graham Gibbs Sue Habeshaw Trevor Habeshaw

53 practical ideas in 7 Chapters:

Essays

Alternative Exams

Assessing Practical And Project Work

Giving Feedback To Students

Objective Tests

Computer-Based Assessment

Criteria

No 4 **53 INTERESTING WAYS OF HELPING YOUR STUDENTS TO STUDY**

Trevor Habeshaw Graham Gibbs Sue Habeshaw

53 practical ideas in 9 Chapters:

Beginning

Reading

Learning With Others

Planning

Taking Notes

Writing

Library Work

Revising

Exams

No 5 **53 INTERESTING COMMUNICATION EXERCISES FOR SCIENCE STUDENTS**

Di Steeds Sue Habeshaw

53 practical ideas in 13 Chapters:

Communication Theory

Study Skills

The Language Of Science

Writing Up Practicals

Writing Instructions

The Arrangement Of Data InTables

Self Presentation

Thinking About Science

Using A Library

Technical Writing

Report Writing

Data Presentation And

Interpretation

Oral Presentations